Anatomical Sketches
Of The Misunderstood

(a scientific guide to surviving
in numbered slides)

Volume II

Also by Joseph D. Reich

If I Told You To Jump Off The Brooklyn Bridge
(Flutter Press, 2009)

A Different Sort of Distance
(Skive Magazine Press, 2010)

Pain Diary: Working Methadone & The Life & Times
Of The Man Sawed In Half (Brick Road Poetry Press, 2010)

Drugstore Sushi (Thunderclap Press, 2010)

The Derivation Of Cowboys & Indians (Fomite Press, 2012)

The Housing Market: a comfortable place to jump off
the end of the world (Fomite Press, 2013)

The Hole That Runs Through Utopia (Fomite Press, 2014)

Taking The Fifth And Running With It: a psychological
guide for the hard of hearing and blind (Broadstone Books,
2015)

The Hospitality Business (Valeviel Press, 2015)

Connecting The Dots To Shangrila: A Postmodern Cultural
Hx Of America (Fomite Press, 2016)

A Case Study Of Werewolves (Fomite Press, 2018)

The Rituals Of Mummification (Sagging Meniscus Press,
2017)

Magritte's Missing Murals: Insomniac Episodes
(Sagging Meniscus Press, 2017)

How To Order Chinese During A Hostage Crisis: Dialects,
Existential Essays, A Play, And Other Poems (Hog Press,
2017)

American Existentialism (Tuba Press, 2017)

An Eccentric Urban Guide To Surviving (Analog Submission Press, 2017)

The American Book Of The Dead (Xi Draconis Books, 2018)

From Premonition To Prophecy (Delinkwent Scholar Press, 2018)

Statutes Of David (Pen & Anvil Press, 2018)

I know why old men sit in front of windows all day sighing & crying & living & dying when the sun goes down on the city at night (Kung-Fu Treachery Press, 2020)

Makeshift Press
114 Wild Rose Circle
Winchester, VA 22602

© 2020 by Joseph D. Reich

All rights reserved. This book or parts thereof may not be reproduced in any form, stored in any retrieval system, or transmitted in any form by any means—electronic, mechanical, photocopy, recording, or otherwise—without prior written permission of the publisher, except as provided by United States of America copyright law. For permission requests, write to the publisher.

Cover art © 2019 by P. Forester
"Love or Confusion" is printed here with permission of P. Forester.

ISBN: 978-1-7341558-1-5

July 2020
MakeshiftPress.org

ANATOMICAL SKETCHES OF THE MISUNDERSTOOD

"Why is it the people who need the most help won't take it?"

-A River Runs Through It

Sneak Performance: Fiddlers & Public Welcome

I was the one they always asked about— I wonder what happened…
well here's an explanation and with a bit of deference and desperation
a presentation so please focus your attention and turn the lights down
low and all gadgets and gizmos off. If you'd like to drink or smoke
please keep it to a minimum and don't make a spectacle as suppose
it's all really about trying to keep that buzz while on the brink like
that bare blinking north star above, so when it all comes down to
the nitty-gritty this is for those girls who believed in me and took
me in when we had nothing and everything to look forward to
beat down and blue, brooding on the outskirts of town, deep
down in the forest; on the lakes and mountains and ocean
beacons minding their own whispering sweet nothings

#1

The life & times of the rabbit in the hat
as you wonder what kind of life is that
(this strange habitat and magic act) just
getting pulled by your ears out of some
big top hat and them clapping like mad
at some uproarious rapturous party
wondering what and where and how
did this happen wanting to creep back
down that long dark rabbit hole and
hide and not be harassed and think
in retrospect how our lives from
beginning to end is just being
taken out against our own
will and volition (trembling,
frightened) having to perform
and meet these ridiculous
expectations not exactly
sure what they want from
you in this absurd thing
called existence (this
big top act) or thing
they like to refer to
as our time on earth

#2

Abracadabra origin and derivation
or maybe just one of those words
in the english language what is it?
onomatopoeia where its definition
sounds exactly like its musical
rhythm suddenly spontaneously
out of the clear blue sky sparking
some sort of revelation and miracle
from all those things in our life that
just makes us want to break down and
cry while instantly healing all our blues
and *melancholia* morphine opium heroin
depending on how pure and what part of
the poppy and how much pain and shame
we're experiencing an instant *panacea* to all
those things that *plague* us in this thing called living

#3

Your life just like one of those shylocks
from the used car lot throwing a surprise
party at your own expense then strapping
you up like some makeshift pinata and with
blindfolds on taking shots at your broken heart.

Completely caught off guard still stripped
down you ask if you can just make a couple
of minor changes to the contract and they tell
you are locked in for the next couple of years

You continue to get these random e-mails
from a jake reno who with all your info
wishes you a happy birthday and if should
ever have any questions or need any kind
of support just feel free to give him a call

Counter/proof(s):

a,

Whenever i hear all of the bullshit statements
of the fake martyrs always claiming having some
thing to do with all their sacrifices, it feels like
some sort of manipulative, premanufactured
reverse-psychology and guilt and brainwash
as some rationalization for why they have
spent their whole lives being a bunch of
cut-throats and hypocrites and not having
a scintilla of morals and ethics, while for
the most part they were the ones who
chose to do what they did (knowing
exactly what they were doing)
or brought kids into the world
and feels more so like having
something to do with their own
self-loathing (fear of death
and living) and mortality

b,

Remember when growing up when parents
in this real pathetic domestic fashion would
start spelling out words so you couldn't
understand them, as you start thinking
about piaget and wittgenstein with their
axioms of having a predisposition for language
and wonder if have one as well for non-verbals?

c,

One of the biggest tragedies is not being
able (for one reason or another) to express
and tell someone how much you really love them
(everything else coming out in some form of bickering)

#4

Every new proclamation and conclusion (and theory)
we come up with stems from the significance of what
we instinctively know and feel and experienced, while
simultaneously our emotional and fragile fear of losing it

#5

After a certain, clear amount of persistent emotional, psychological, and spiritual abuse, people's self-image as well as physiological system does become hardwired (fragile and more vulnerable) toward traits and characteristics and specific symptoms of depression due to all that trauma and damage, more often than not, tend to take it out on themselves, becoming 'self-fulfilling' even self-destructive but if they can at least just realize and identify when these selfsame repetitive images and instances happen, as well as triggers to those resulting cognitive and behavioral patterns and manifestations of such emotions as rage and self-hatred and guilt and conflict, almost owe it to themselves over a specific period (having paid their dues and developed insight and wisdom) to try and turn it around and find some kind of peace, solace, and happiness in their life

#6

The real sign of intelligence— being an intellect
is being receptive, open-minded, compassionate
and sympathetic; most of them, paradoxically
are too ignorant, prejudiced, and know-it-alls
(thus not knowing themselves) in fact, ironically
preventing the ability and potential towards any sort
of growth, learning, wisdom, intuition and the senses
presenting as confused, conflicted, defensive, hostile

Intellectualization represents also 'a fear of intimacy'
and a hell of a lot of role-playing (and self-interest)
while not by coincidence rarely are these people
anywhere to be found when most needed

#7

Whenever a family member or acquaintance
tells me of one those people with a good reputation
after i meet them often think did i get the right person?

Those always talking of good judgment
seem like the ones furthest away from it

#8

Peace is the panacea for the human beast
we invent things like police (po-leeeze!)
politics and preachers to keep these
inhabitants at ease; a med for not
hanging our self on a daily basis

An old asian couple moves
to an island with no people
to try and raise pigs
and tangerine trees

#9

I.

Dear gertrude (both queen & hotelier)

whenever i use words like honestly honestly
i'm not being honest only if i maybe happen
to think (or maybe may be) about honesty
to honestly be honest see? and reasons
to be or not not not to be as honestly
just creeping and trying to get through
these days trying to get out of this daze
honestly if honestly i was an orange tree

the weather in england...

(is a pretty middle-aged woman
in a purple suede dress her pawn
shop crown getting fixed wit
crumpet & cream complexion
and buttock of bread pudding
leftover in pudding dish
during all that boredom
in a downpour of drizzle)

paris just as faraway as cuba...

(as a fig meant of your imagination
finally at last with no return address
a dress made up of printemps sir
la rive droite and having no set time
to show up and return home to your
apartement with a view through your
shutters of her undressing and a piece of
jesus' broken heart buried in sacre-couer)

surviving
off vietnamese
brie & baguette
ripe for the taking...

II.

Just Like The Languid & Lazy…

imagine rooms available with no hotel
your own personal streetcar which just
reads "vacancy" or wasted version of eternity
which rattles blissfully past the exhibitionist
mausoleums and procession of malyasian
peasants on hands and knees in bamboo
hats manicuring the perfect plush grass
which splits the pristine luxurious avenue
in half with all your past girlfriends laid
out on the ancient marble steps in the form of
phantoms of overgrown antebellum mansions
madwomen making their daily rounds in the
sweltering cobblestone in the wild abandonment
of what it means to be terribly lonely somewhere
between toulouse & bourbon & the mississippi
shattered river queen mysteriously rolling by
keeping all mystical secrets to itself on the sly
insane effeminate hustlers and their long-lost
sons not believing a word coming out of them
angels telling you your future at the lemonade
stand on mad undulating lawns with a history
of bloodshed in the midst of torrential downpour
and the only scent that thick magnolia which
penetrates practically every pore of your being
making you want to just break down and weep
poor wailing black boys very dramatically
threaten to stab each other with pencils
after school as you return home alone
with all these strange stirring spirits
lingering in you for suicidal supper
and dreaming of your future…

III.

On The Opposite Of War

a drifter dressed in disguise dressed in black & white top hat & tails
spying two gorgeous young girls to die for playing on pink tennis courts
spying a flat-chested nude sunbather having been excommunicated
& now an eager expatriate looking forward to starting a new life
of seduction along the rocky shores of the mediterranean
spying a brash drowning victim showing off talking way
too loudly already with his press corps & parades &
townsmen not sure whether to hang or stone him
spying a ghostly hotelier just as haunted by his past as his future
spying a lonesome lone traveler with no direction pleasantly wailing
behind the azure shutters of a half-crazed mansion on the border
of anarchist countries with black roses growing all around it
spying a young vagabond fast asleep perfectly contented
with his head leaned up against his shofar in the cobblestone alley
spying lesbian sisters going at it one giving birth to a domineering
mother & the other to a poor old docile submissive father figure
spying a clown & his whole clown family in a state of mourning
reading different parts of the paper muted around the breakfast table
spying a black moon sitting on top of a white picket fence her hitting
you over the head with a paper while confessing how much you love
her listening to roy orbison dropping missiles on all of culture &
civilization 'do not pass go do not collection 200' to know
so much really does 'depend on a red wheelbarrow' filled
with shattered milk bottles & carcasses of broken dolls
spying an aristocratic housewife trying to keep up as much with the
expectations of her father as she pretends not to with the neighbors
spying a delinquent kid running away from the mailbox on a mission
hollering out loud–"i got it!" not caring who sees or catches him
spying the town idiot & town genius both with limited modes
of functioning simply sulking all day on the corner with dumb
founded expressions eavesdropping on the foghorns
spying a suicidal barber passed-out in his barber chair
with cloak & dagger in a real-life version of truth or dare
spying a harlequin picking up the shattered bones
of a stray dog he once loved & trying to piece them
all back together again one by one by one by one

spying bad boys playing cards within the shelter of shadows
beneath some bridge gathered around a table of girl scout cookies
spying a bunch of young clean-cut military men trying to con
a whole clan of kids innocently taking lunch in the cafeteria
spying a pimp with his glowing electric crucifix one part to store
drugs & other to keep lists of people who owe him & a sport's
jersey which reads on the back "don't shoot the messenger"
spying a funeral director very formally dressed
selling tombstones half-off
spying a whole mountain with just a side full of tree
stumps on your way to a resort of brokendown
motels to meet lovers on the off-season ocean
spying portosans being transported on the back of flatbeds
racing down the highway to the boardwalk on the sea
along with beer & ice cream & seafood & freaks
spying that immaculate biway running from the suburbs to the sea
one side of idiots rushing to their wedding & the other to get their
clean/cut divorces both pretty much guilty of originally doing the
exact same thing while in the middle the old timers or even worse
old money taking their time taking it all for granted because they
can afford it & purchased one of those very exclusive pre-payed
passes, while never once had to pay their dues & be the exact
ones who would run you over with one of those exclusive cowardly
grins knowing daddy's lawyer will always bail them out instantly
turning their sins to virtue & back again as never gets mentioned
spying a boy simply sitting in his bedroom fidgeting & fooling
around with the channels of his ham radio which will
decide the fate of the free world
spying the weather woman simply weeping in silhouette
behind the blinds like some ancient weathervane worn
by time right on top a widow watch
spying teenage nymphomaniacs putting on their act
pacing back & forth in front of lit lattices keeping
boys at bay literal ghosts of former selves
spying a cross-dressing wedding couple dressed
in drag & the father simply strewn out in his
suburban backyard reading the sunday paper
spying the groom instantly falling in love
with the girls in the coat closet & the bride
with the fine young shy gigolo cousin training pigeons
spying the peculiar projectionist nodding-out in the dark
in the hypnotic tick-tock of the grandfather clock just

as content to collect his pension as his bundle of dope
spying a whole line of silent hysterical rockettes kicking
their legs up in unison setting the whole ballroom on fire
claiming bridesmaids blackmailed them & made them do it
spying a lamplighter living a double triple & multiple lives
just as satisfied smoking a butt in the sweltering night some
where between the movie theaters missions prisons & churches
spying the widow innkeeper grinning with a pained expression
holding up a different variety of rabbits by their ears in ceremonial
succession while this ridiculous routine & ritual implying that will
be their supper spying a middle-aged man reenacting his whole life
ending it by decorating & casually lighting all of the lonely desolate
curtains of the home on fire starting like some strange dream while
ending like some holy nightmare

#10

Our breakthroughs and revelations bloom
from simple sudden metaphors and images

#11

I've never been a big believer in those who believed
it was avant-garde or bohemian to turn away from
certain art movements while turning towards others
as seemed to me these people just as guilty or absurd
(with this selfsame collective herd mentality) in the need for
rebelling, while to me should not art be viewed individually
and intimately in what 'moves me' and brings about certain
memories and meaning, or even motivates me toward a
whole other form of imagination 'of believing and being'
similar perhaps to the ridiculous, age old debate and futile
sacrifice and slaughter all in the name of organized religion

#12

a,

That statement 'contrary to popular opinion'
always to me has been a real strange, perplexing
and obvious one as if break down and deconstruct
it, all my beliefs and aspirations have always been
contrary to popular opinion; even think of that term
'popular' (and say it out loud) and how absurd and
ridiculous it all sounds, while go back to your youth
and adolescence and all those cruel and brutal erratic
behaviors and contradictions usually coming from
some of the biggest backstabbers and hypocrites
while in retrospect, think i feel pretty comfortable
and confident in being contrary to popular opinion

b,

Most forms of stability seem to lack stability
based on their shallow premise towards attention
seeking, even advertising alienating (it is with
a sense of "nausea" and nihilism of the feelings
and senses that we experience this) and appears
to often be just for those few and lucky born into
it or those wise or insightful enough to experience
it individually and appreciate it for the fleeting
aesthetic moment as a passing phase to be stored
spiritually in the long-term sensibilities of the psyche

c,

The greatest gift for the poet and philosopher
(thief and scholar) is to not be taken seriously
during their childhood (forced to constantly
act-out and get into a hell of a lot of trouble
to establish an identity) continuing to be
doubted even when they get older learning

to cope and survive and get by (wearing different disguises including 'the gift of gab' and picking up behavioral patterns) in practically every economic strata

#13

Proclamations:

0, Too many will try to turn you into a mug shot
   into an exact replica and likeness-image that
   they project of their own self-hatred, while
   it is simply your job to break the mold of how
   they framed you and taken you out of context

1, It's crucial and significant to remember your original
   feeling and instinct after a specific statement has been
   made, as opposed to all that unnecessary brooding and
   fixating which more times than not materializes thereafter
   (while in fact actually backfires on an empirical, emotional,
   psychological, and spiritual level, as more likely a trigger
   to some previous form of abuse and damage that has gone
   unresolved) and only proves how the dynamic and defense
   mechanism of intense self-reflection or intellectualization
   not always so accurate (sometimes takes on the form
   of opposites) to the original, core, primal emotion

   being so tough on yourself or brow-beating not always
   so productive, or better yet stated constantly doubting
   yourself becomes something of 'a crime against man'

2, Those constantly doing good deeds and preaching
   virtue often turn out to be rather incomplete people
   full of hypocrisies and contradictions so quick to
   pass judgment and be impulsive and not quite as
   open-minded and 'liberal' welcoming and receptive
   to those they deem to be (or not be) part of their circle

3, The unreliable (those who never keep their word
   or follow through) just eventually end up draining
   the fuck out of you, while ironically not really so much
   the ones you cared about (or thought about) in the first place

4, Who would ever really want to try to fit in and be accepted
and a part of the whole 'exclusive' country club environment?
what ridiculous aspirations having the desperate need to seek
such approval and "reputations" and a piece of the illusion!
i've seen people literally slave their whole lives just to try
and reach such heights to obtain this lifestyle and how many
people they have felt the need to slight; to alienate and belittle
and battle to reach this absurd goal and status acting like pseudo-
gods having no idea rather they're the biggest (tiniest) devils

i guess in fact true it's all in the details...

5, Why are the intellectuals always
the first ones to laugh the first
ones to clap as if they were
the first ones to get it and
know so much more than
everyone but not quite
enough to be up there
at the podium and when
it's all over are no better
than any tourist who all
took the exact same picture
because they could afford it

6, People are always trying to test each other's
mortality to try and prove how immortal they
are which only proves the morons they are

7, Looking back to your past before there was even a past
you wore masks to see how long you could make it last

8, You've loved some of them and suppose
some of them have loved you too
while in looking back that there
clearly is a form of truth

9, Watch out! they might just not get or have
any idea how you're trying to show your love
which in the long-run makes you feel awfully alone

10, There is very little within the boundaries of reality
that can equal the fantastic borders of the imagination

11, There's such a fine line between the thief
and comedian with an obsessive need to
please and release the pressures and burdens
from the everyday struggle and suffering of society

12, Of course there's the whimsy and impulsivity
contradictions and hypocrisies of human nature
but to me, those who deliberately make others
feel guilty seems something of a sin for all the damage
and conflict it inflicts on the human spirit and eventually
brings to the functioning of the core identity and psyche

13, How do you not break hearts with your heart already broken
along with everything else they want and expect from you?

14, Your life or existence a prison sentence
in how they treat you or don't treat you
and never follow through and suppose
all it comes down to is just paying
your dues and somehow finding a way
of making it through without killing
yourself or all the things and people
around you; maybe even through those
dark dusty blinds seeing the wildflowers
growing on the hill, drizzle on the red canoe

15, Only these days if you get out resembling
a 'live human being' (always open to debate)
they'll ask such insane survey-like questions

like please tell us about your stay? is there anything
we could have done to improve our services? on a
scale from 1-10 please rate your rate of rehabilitation?
any suggestions for extra-curricular activities? for
the co's? for the social workers? for the warden?

16, (fill in the empty spaces...)

    proper protocol for how to placate the public

    reduce their high-expressed emotion

    get them back to baseline to maintain
    a steady rapport and communication

    for purposes of engagement and to make
    a connection provide heaps of validation

    use such phrases like i see
    where that can be frustrating

    i can see where you are angry

    what can i do to make you happy?

    once again i want to extend an apology on behalf

    once you have reduced rate of anger and frustration
    and returned back to a baseline of civil discourse
    and communication and customer has been
    perfectly placated go on to sell product

    ask if there is any other way you can be of assistance

    again provide your quota of sincere sorry's and thank them
    again for continuing to 'patronize' and being a good customer

17, The one thing i learned the real hard way
   in the hospitality field or hotel business
   (graveyard shift most especially) is that

life's just one big fucken absurd circus
and the guests (sexless, or those of
complete decadence) who don't make
complete idiots and imbeciles and
spectacles of themselves without
conflict with the front desk and
bellmen and in-house security
i guess in a half-crazed way
are the ones we consider
to be the 'upstanding
citizens' of society

18, People when you first meet them
always seem to feel this obligation
to act so formal (with all their formalities
thinking this is what makes them so polite
and well-mannered) yet actually just always
made me feel more so uncomfortable in my
own skin and couldn't really make a connection
or even for that matter not really trust them…
matter of fact believed far more in the hustler
(with his experience and wisdom) 'cause
at least you knew what you were getting
as long as you kept an eye on him

19, Once you clearly know somebody's thought-pattern
(and personality) you pretty much can figure out
all of their moves (and motives) with their active
pettiness and backstabbing even though it's really
the last thing you care to know and be around and
a part of and honestly prefer not to be involved with

20, "The rebel" does not know any different and just doing
the best that he can to make it. the artist or raconteur would
like to have you think otherwise and had some choice in the
matter (or ulterior motive) or even for that matter to evoke a
reaction but mostly purely instinctive and primal and doing

the best with the cards that he's been dealt more
often than not coming from a place of hurt and
pain and profound desperation and damage

21, All of those things that we dream about for our future
(those instinctive images and visions and selfsame
intuition) did not come by coincidence and becomes
our eventual baseline for truth and reality and state of mind

22, Has it ever been said i have regrets about my future
well if not then why say it about our past
if in fact we really tried our best?

23, Certain such phrases like 'in good faith' never really
seemed (or came from a place) to be in good faith

24, Often context is used as a criteria or standard of judgment
as proof or evidence but if look too deeply into it can have
the opposite effect and bring about confusion and conflict

25, One should not have to ask the intellectual linguistic
question about if it's satirical or symbolic? ironic?
allegorical or some sort of parable? that almost
becomes irrelevant; it either is or it isn't, and can
assure you was written out of a certain sense of necessary
desperation and the sheer hypocrisies of human nature

26, It becomes a strange and perplexing illusion how we so
often appear to get betrayed by the impulsive and inaccurate
uses and abuses of language (meant to violate and cause
pain) as opposed to the actual psychological dynamic
(of the origins from which it all emanated) that we find
so maddening (of stubbornness, ignorance, and rigidity)
and then eventually after everything settles, cursed with
those extraneous overwhelming emotions and feelings
of confusion and conflict

Addendum: love/hate sonnets

They always seem to rule out suicide
and say idiotic obvious things like
seemed so happy and was turning
his life around but it seems to me
from what i've seen a pattern more
likely that that day just had the guts
to finally do it after living a life where
he felt like he was constantly suffering
dying practically on a day by day basis

We get through this life seeing and processing
it not just by a primary but also a parallel and
perpendicular point-of-view and perspective

How revelations come upon you so
all of a sudden and wonder what took
you so long through all the suffering?

If in fact opposites attract (in form and function and aesthetics)
then likewise by no coincidence it shouldn't surprise you on
some parallel plane similar forms and images and memories
and meaning of resemblance so often bring about
such conflicting and confusing conclusions

Why is it always those who make such
conclusions you've come full circle come
from the biggest squares and feels like some
grand triangulation of some eternal game
of truth or dare desperately searching for
that starting place where it all began

Anytime i heard one of those pompous professors
or even peers or acquaintances suddenly declare
like they came upon some great revelation–

"it begs the question" my original instinct
and reaction was why would anyone or anything
beg the question probably most likely just got
to some point in their existence where they got
sick of all the bullshit and just didn't want to be
bothered anymore anonymous left the hell alone
i mean who the hell would want to be surrounded
by one of those know-it-alls who begs the question?

        Almost everything i was mandated to apologize
        for as a kid (i take back with great conviction)
        as made perfect impulsive sense against all
        those aloof and arrogant asshole adults who
        were not quite as honorable as they thought
        more so humorless trying to steal
        my spirit and everything i worked
        so hard for trying to put me at a loss

When those you turn to make you turn elsewhere
i swear this life can just get awfully lonesome

        We sometimes in lovers hope to somehow find
        friends and in friends strangers who won't judge us

We always seem to fall in love when we're lost
somewhere on the fringe ironically not too far from
the original sin composed of dream fantasy wish imagination

        A thief's life seems like
        shangrila with no return address

Can ghosts be passed down from generation to generation?

> If i had it all over to do again
> i wouldn't be a pain in the ass
> and burden and say if i had it
> all over to do again as usually
> those are the types who would
> do it exactly the same and
> keep on torturing you with
> if i had it all over to do again

That philosophical question—"does the means justify the ends?"
is when it feels like there's just no end if you know what i mean
and a complete loss of justification eventually engaging in a self-
inflicted vicious abuse cycle, while often satire becomes the only
real surreal palpable metaphor (parable) and maddening solution

> I wish all those assholes would just
> get off their cellphones as does anyone
> remember the art of conversation? culture?
> and if in fact desperation "is" the mother of
> invention, or however that saying's supposed
> to go i'm gonna invent one with electrodes
> to get us back to the original instinct and core

Battles are constantly having to be chosen
(in a world of aggressiveness and acting-out
and jealousy and pettiness) in order to eventually
become a wise man, but never brought on by your
self so is not wisdom as much an act of cognition and
courage and conviction, perseverance and perception
even learned and acquired (inherited) as it is inherent?

> Surrealism, where the feeling
> (and image) means more
> than the definition

That fight or flight syndrome
is very much the manifestation

and difference (and likeness)
of our dreams and nightmares

                To me it seems like i just need to get
                closure over my fucked-up dreams
                my reality, i did a long time ago

The child of a narcissist who his
whole life has had his identity stolen
from him (with practically no self-image
and persistent sense of self-loathing and
lack of meaning and purpose, almost having
a love/hate relationship with 'the self') will
end up feeling so spiritually neglected, cheated
and taken advantage, as well as so traumatized
and damaged, not even aware of this selfsame
dynamic and just ends up through a psychodynamic
of 'self-fulfilling prophecy' developing self-destructive
behavior (severely at-risk with a cognitive disconnect
even at times suicidal ideations) following parallel
'acting-out' behavioral patterns concomitant with that
lack of identity of killing himself in one form or another;
will in fact be made to feel (not feel) like he does not exist at
all on an emotional, psychological, and spiritual level, while those
'at risk' acting-out behaviors very similar to one who self-mutilates
for purposes of pain and pleasure without even being aware of it

                Did anyone ever go up to freud
                and refer to him as freudian
                kafka as kafkaesque
                plato as platonic
                as most likely were
                just trying to get through
                this life of pain and suffering
                and figure it all out through
                self-analysis and parables

With all the constant suffering and pain
on a daily basis truths end up feeling
like falsehoods as you psychologically
forget their foundation and basis like
when you repeat a word or phrase over
and over again and loses its significance
(meaning and purpose) until sometimes
all you can really do is just turn to music

        Why does it often seem the trigger to the trigger
        to the trigger to the trigger actually in fact seems
        more hurtful and painful than the original violation
        (perhaps a fear of the unknown *and* known) and
        that now the fragile (and damaged vulnerable)
        mind (and body and soul) has had time to think
        and reflect about it as opposed to those original
        primitive and primal instincts (and defenses)
        of coping and survival mechanisms, and now
        presents as something of a real-life nightmare
        (which has been embedded in the subconscious)
        and haven't exactly quite gotten complete closure
        —such shattered souls! thinking of starting one
        of those snowglobe collections…

I love my wife because she cannot save me
and wouldn't even know where to start but
still has that cute sing-songy voice which
i suppose is the only thing that matters.
i once had a girlfriend (who had just been
through a miserable 7 year marriage) who
said she loved me because she knew there
were certain places she could not get close

I guess i fall somewhere in the middle…

        Experience, suffering, humility
        is what eventually makes
        the individual complete

Constantly glamorizing is a strange
paradoxical form of lamenting
or state of denial about
our present day life

        Most *bad boys* got their start
        from those with far less heart(s)
        and when you meet their guardian
        says such stuff like–"charmed i'm
        sure" and ain't sure if they're being
        real or rhetorical and see why they
        really had no other choice but
        to put on and play such roles

"The night is still young"
who came up with that one?

        Those incapable of telling the truth
        are really just a bunch of false hoods

Most romantics got
their start on sinking ships

        The sudden throbbing blast and wail of foghorns
        out of nowhere like a great big rag being thrown
        over your weary broken bones to instantly help
        to forgive & forget & heal & save your soul

Those days i guess when felt happy to be alive
nowadays seems like just fighting off dying

        Everyday should be a prison riot
        against this life sentence called reality

Why at weddings does it seem like they're always
trying to impart this wisdom, while at funerals on
their best behavior? i don't know— doesn't it just
seem like it should be the other way around and
coming from those just acting-out, resentful,
drained, leftover, and not particularly sound?
the grand metaphor for 'who you know' as
those who have developed the reputation for
'virtue' or 'soul' some of the biggest assholes

        If only white people (tourists) in suburban amerika
        picked up nicer and kinder body language and
        affectations but unfortunately for the most part
        (in a cookie-cutter, homogeneous manner) act
        like it's some sort of honor to be around them
        and own and control everything around them

Those with some of the most profound disorders
say some of the most profound things...

        I am confident that i have lost all confidence
        in confidence which is all simply just a bullshit
        illusion invented by the human species (to try
        and assert their dominance) and that type always
        way too loud for their own good obnoxious obscene
        and opinionated and wish just once could turn down
        their volume and all of their false knowledge about
        people and things they know absolutely nothing about

All the times i have had to be so diplomatic
with people who were not even close to worth
it (matter of fact absurdly impulsive and barbaric)
the scholars and philosophers such as nietzsche
and machiavelli over time have spoken in depth
about the 'might over right' concept while deep
down instinctively knowing this dynamic and
in an almost opposite way (from experience

and wisdom) have had to do the opposite
based on this inherent trait of human nature

        I've put far more stock in strangers
        as opposed to those i have become
        way too familiar who have a tendency
        (through proven behavioral patterns)
        to naturally skew the facts and figures
        not follow through on any of their offers
        and in a down 'right' dirty manner flatter
        while thus find i so much more prefer and
        feel comfortable and put trust in that age-old
        adage and its results "don't talk to strangers"

Be very careful! they'll treat you like a second-class citizen
even when you're doing it well. they don't seem to very much
like people of this ilk. jealousy's a bitch and pathetically makes
them real angry and hostile turning that existential statement on
its head 'i think therefore i am' trying to make you so depressed
don't care or give a damn whether you are alive or you are dead

If it is you or it is them…

        That lazy cliche expression having the patience
        of a saint could never fully picture or imagine
        as most of them just seemed more like who you
        knew and having some kind of connection, while
        real saints in my opinion are just the ones who
        cope and deal with all the maddening futile
        bullshit and betrayal and hypocrisies and
        contradictions on a daily basis, and end up
        becoming more patients than any saint i ever
        saw desperately trying to make it and go it
        alone and rise above; too much patience
        makes you do some really crazy stuff…

Socrates (plato, buddha) nietzsche, diaphanes
how do you ask a liar to stop lying (to you)?
you can keep on proving them wrong but
in the long-run becomes draining and honestly
where does that really get you? all you can really
do is move on to some better and higher 'form' of truth

    Honestly never been a big believer in belief
    cause right when you start believing there's
    always something which instantly makes
    you betray those beliefs like all of selfish
    and phony humanity which rarely seems to
    contain one single trait or characteristic of faith
    or 'humanity' and so when all those infamous
    scholars or teachers ask you to speak of your
    beliefs cannot really take them too seriously
    (even though they appeared idealistically
    well-intended but lacking in the merit of life
    experience) as never very much believed in
    them as well when really stop to think about it

Every time i had some fine girl on my arm
and for the first time in so long was finally
feeling a certain sense of liberation and freedom
having good independent thoughts would suddenly
burst out with something real nauseating and gross
like–"penny for your thoughts" and ironically
not by coincidence, not sure why, instantly
felt this overwhelming sense of loss and broke

        Tourists contaminate and defeat the purpose
        of culture while i prefer when i really
        get to not know them…

Where are the libraries where they'll
all just shut the fuck up? find i want to just
shoosh the librarians as well who also don't get it

There is no longer silence
in american cinema anymore
like richard burton & elizabeth
taylor eternally going at it, like
satire turned inside-out unsure of
the difference between fact & fiction

I never really understood
that one 'all's fair in love and war'
as love's got nothing to do with war
and war sure as hell nothing to do with love...
is this the one where opposites attract, as always had
my most profound relationships in crisis and state of flux

        I swear i have seen women, wives
crawling slowly in cars all the way
out to faraway boardwalks on the sea
what exactly they wanted or seeking
far deeper than anything they could
possibly fathom in their shallow being
melancholy, bleak (almost disassociating
as if in a slow-death state of mourning
developing a whole other identity
without necessarily even being aware
of it) looking for younger men on a mission
in the missions and meat markets of the city
and felt such a pity (could see it in their
eyes) wondering why they were so lost
and far-gone and looking for younger
guys, while this felt so impulsive and
not romantic, but then thought about the nature
of man and those i've known with their know-
it-all demeanor, never asking or talking about
anyone else but themselves, and then could
see why they were so lowdown, down-in-the-
dumps, miserable; their form of literal 'attention-
seeking' seeking some form of love and sense of
being and belonging, and now instantly could see...

I think when you break up with women
(or vice-versa) you also end up breaking
up with their bodies, while of course
there's that whole 'empty bed syndrome'
(and profound triggers of emptiness,
desertion and abandonment) not just
because you miss their presence and
being (and all that companionship and
spiritual things which of course holds
deep meaning on an emotional and also
chemical level) but everything else you
miss such as their shape and form and
figure (an intimate object-permanence)
without being aware of it which you
have grown so accustomed and gotten
so used to (made you feel excited, vibrant
and alive) and likewise becomes hardwired

                All that pain and pressure turned to instant pleasure
                with your object of affection (your perceived loved
                one) becoming confused and conflicted by this
                instant-gratification and quasi-savior (sometimes
                even feelings of guilt and a little hostile in what
                they want from you) about what we think love is
                with all the brutal draining things life does to you

Looking back at those relationships
with a major sexual component
one of the few times in life
i have absolutely no regrets
as lust was the literal act of
to 'forgive and forget' and
isn't that just a lot of what
love is? the keen sensation
of feeling completely content?

                First love gives the 'impression' and resemblance
                of the concept of the emotion of pure happiness
                experiencing the sensation where all burdens

> (and tension and pressure) are relieved and a
> freedom and liberation of the senses, while all
> moments of time and tenses come together in
> the 'here and now' of the past present and future
> with orgasm and a sudden rush of pleasure while
> all's forgotten and forgiven and must be what love is

In high school if you were lucky enough to get
lucky fooling around was always so primal and
physical and romantic and wild; out-of-control
contorted geometric figures taking on different
positions and forms in the back seats of cars, or
strangers suddenly become familiar and turned-
on in some sibling's darkened bedroom at some
keg party; that volunteer from the audience
who goes missing in a magic act giving off
the illusion of lost then just like that found

> All really beautiful women lie a little
> and if happen to call them out on it
> will naturally back themselves up
> with another one which gives them
> all their beauty and humor and charm
>
> that expression–"je ne sais quois"
> did not just come out of nowhere

I used to live with this girl in the village
who dressed up mannequins for a living
while got dumped by her boyfriend for
a younger woman. i won't begin to tell you
about her passive-aggressive behavior and
her on & off explosions and how it all ended.
when she found out where i ended up moving
right around the corner she used to stroll back
and forth on the weekend beneath her parasol like
some psychotic seduction thinking i'd get turned on

        Marriage is some sort of mirage mirror image
        mixed feelings of mistaken identity monster
        mutely howling in the midst of a monsoon
        battle of the sexes newlywed game family
        feud they never listen to you lifetime bid
        when's i gonna get out on good behavior
        not sure if jesus would have made it and
        forced to go back on the preaching circuit

I wrote a letter to myself
today saying "i miss you"
but didn't know what to
say cuz have no feelings
for me as think prefer it
more so from those border
line girls who are gonna just pick
up and leave for no particular reason

        Baby when you used to cry
        thinking i was gonna leave
        you never knew how deep
        was the damage of what
        your parents did to you
        and at that moment knew
        how much i loved you
        and whatever happened
        knew i wouldn't leave
        you till my dying day

Going to sleep with a tear
in your eye wanting to
break down and cry
is just another form
of still waters run deep

        Somewhere between yonkers & the bronx
        is a broken heart— love is wanting to
        put back together those broken parts

#14

It's weird— looking back at my life those who played the role of being real down-to-earth and humble soul full and sincere honestly never once kept their word

dishonesty's a bad thief, obvious and predictable…

#15

One should not waste
their formative years
simply shooting for
good grades as will
find ironically cheating
themselves (turning a phrase
turning that cliche on its head).
i never wanted to be a leader
but was content being a wise
ass keeping them in stitches
as those in my opinion
were the ones far more
sincere and committed
sensitive holy and sacred
spending my after school
hours involved in extra
curricular activities
like detention where i found
out that cute tomboy to die
for from the grade below
had a crush on me and that
meant more to me and really
believed in that age old belief
trouble always seems to find
me and forced me to see a shrink
where he always wanted to test
me to prove how smart i was and
subconsciously didn't want to to
prove how much i wasn't until i
eventually proved with my sixth
sense and spirit how he would
break my trust and confidence

Proof:

Can how they always appear to process you wrong
(and project their own fucked-up shit) be interpreted
like that philosopher dyaphones spending his whole
existence trying to find one honest man and never could
find one? almost every thief i have known had a heart
of gold who in fact really wanted to contribute something
positive (and be a part of) to his culture and environment
but knew because of fate (and all the fucked-up ways
and damage from how he grew up) realistically futilely
just could not and decided somewhere down the line to
take back and steal (to try and make a connection) and
make it all his own

#16

I always found it so perverse and paradoxical
using such words like "innocent" and "guilty"
to decide one's fate while if apply it to the psycho-
logical and spiritual term and genre, one who feels
'constantly guilty' often emanating from a profoundly
pure 'innocent soul' but when the courts and court system
get involved and mangle and distort and institutionalize
it takes on a whole other completely different meaning
in linguistics, even bordering on the absurd, whether to
make the determination of 'guilty' or 'innocent' and at
best get a 3-5 bid with a chance of parole (while the guilty
and innocent soul goes through the constant thought pattern
and psychodynamic of desperately seeking approval, which
ironically puts them in something of a repetitive, existential
prison finding it virtually impossible to break out of taking it
out on themselves and inextricably becoming self-destructive)
and if somehow find a way of holding on long enough and
show a certain amount of patience and perseverance (keeping
'out of trouble' with how they try to break you and make you
feel about yourself) finally at last break out and get out of this
maddening, futile cycle of self-loathing and doubt all based
on 'good behavior,' as this will be your proverbial form of
freedom and liberation, while the lumber trucks keep on rolling
back and forth between mountains and the season; past the pool
halls and motels and diners, as all you care about at last in the
here and now is a simple warm cup of java and a girl to call
your own like some fallen angel you can finally rely on and
love, a clean motel room with simply a phone and tub and her
to fall back on; the innocent and guilty spooning one another
which feels something like a whole lifetime lasting
all the way through the night right into the dawn

#17

They say man has a predisposition for language
well then what would be the shrug of a shoulder?

(a temper-tantrum? feeling constantly guilty? indifference?
fleeting suicide ideations? the change of seasons? purchasing
make-up gifts from the back of those gourmet food catalogs?)

Proof:

Those bar-mitzvahs back in the seventies
when barbra streisand sang–"it's raining
it's pouring, my love life is boring me to
tears after all these years…" while at the
disco with your white boy afro started slow
dancing all of course ending with some real
melodramatic boogying and donna summer
chiming in "enough is enough is enough!"
as nice jewish girls started pointing and
wagging their fingers at you even then
not understanding all the drama and what it
was you possibly could have done to deserve this?

#18

One wonders if when jesus was weeping
on the cross and was like his fellow jew
houdini who-did-it being something of
an escape artist and took off would we
in fact have anything resembling the
industry of organized religion with all
of its present day issues and problems?

It's ironic with the nature of man
how well we did with organized crime

Proof:

Jesus hangs like an old tarnished lighting fixture
off the wall of a decrepit atlantic city hotel

Dummy-ventriloquist act shows up
to the funeral to give the eulogy to
all the really bad supporting actors

#19

People flatter themselves thinking you want
to hang with them (rather hang myself) while
honestly never even crossed my mind or gave
a damn as just a naturally, curious, inquisitive
and generous soul, and ironically i swear got
no idea how much more you value your peace
(of mind) and privacy and time on earth, and
all those little, solitary things in life which
make you content and allow you to be alone

Proof:

They always want to do such stuff like go to bars
and strip clubs poetry readings lectures while to
me they all seem like the exact same thing and
always end up feeling the exact same feeling
of excruciatingly lonely and think what lost
souls they must have to be to want to do such
things and just like those crazy keg parties back
in high school standing in some pal's damp drizzly
chilly fallen leaf backyard awkward getting buzzed
not even yet liking the taste of beer and trying to
charm some girl you never even thought of before
and if by some miracle you happen to score always
have to see her the following monday in school
forced to have to explain yourself (while everything
silly having become so serious) almost like pleading
temporary insanity feeling as much the victim as the thief

#20

You can sometimes see why people might become atheists
'cause there are just so many constant goddamn injustices
and bullshit you have to deal with on a daily basis so many
cowards and clowns and conflicts imbeciles and idiots who
seem to be running the whole goddamn system sometimes
feels like it's just some evil accountant who has absolutely
no accountability playing around and manipulating figures
or some life insurance agent who just won't return your
call how these days they now require you to get referrals
but the nursing staff always gets it wrong and translates
the exact opposite to your omniscient all-knowing doctor
you're no longer allowed to even talk to and then these
are the institutions ringing your fucking phone can see
why people turn to drugs to weed and opiates and drinking
to cheating and gambling and other forms of instant-gratification

can see where disney and i.b.m.
have fallen about a quarter point

here come the holidays…commercials
for luxury cars and exotic men's cologne

Ms. Munchausen (and abuses of power)

dx #1

Those in the quote on quote medical profession
who pass instant judgment and make diagnoses
(in things they have not been trained in nor have
absolutely no competence or compassion) about
issues you did not even go in there for (while in fact
went in there out of your own self-motivation to try
and improve yourself) make you walk out doubting
and questioning yourself and proportionately lonelier
and more hostile clearly having taken on the roles of false
gods otherwise known as an acute form of abuse of power

dx #2

Can you imagine a freaking nurse or doctor
who never fucken listens and swear keeps
on prescribing you the wrong medication
and this is your supposed support system
and multiple times constantly has the same
wrong clinic continually calling you up like
some fucked-up crank phone call demented
game of telephone and you end up just taking
your frustration out on them and these are the
competent professionals bastions institutions
of which we are required to get a referral and
yes my dear this is what real satire is made of.
remember i told you about that film "the hunger"
when david bowie was just sitting and waiting forever
in the waiting room at his doctors and had this disease
where you age out of proportion rapidly and when the
doctor finally came to get him he had become a very
old man and hollered something along the lines i told
you this would happen i told you not to keep me waiting!

Online on their site like being some kind of furniture
shop or used car lot tells you got voted the #1 practice
and wonder what that award ceremony looked like and
who were the judges and who took second and honorable mention?

Wonder what their rating was for the complaint department?

dx #3

You wonder why you just want to put a bullet in your brain
...suffering from arthritic pain...you get a call in the middle
of the day which exclaims in this mechanical high-pitched
insane voice–"hi...this is daisy...we see you are looking
for other healthcare opportunities" and still your primary
has not even followed through with the original referral

m.

I am sincerely finding myself very frustrated with your services
or lack there of...i explained in depth and with respectful clarification
about your referral never getting faxed. i was assured it was and
followed through with you providing me their phone number to
make the appointment myself, which of course i'm always happy
to do so and contribute in any way i can. h. claimed she never received
any fax at all from your office and just something from last year and
told me she was just going to call your practice (without providing any
specific explanation to why she was) in reference to a rheumotology
appointment. of course i have not heard back from her or from your
practice. i had explained to you and to her that in fact i did cancel
an appointment last year because most likely i was just very over
whelmed with so many appointments literally all over vermont as
well as dartmouth-hitchcock. the patient, in my opinion, if they are
doing their due diligence has every right to, whether dealing with
family crises or something as simple as not having transportation
or some other reason out of their own autonomy and will and volition
as long as they are clearly communicating that they can't make it. m.,
this has developed something of an absurd satirical and kafkaesque
quality as i simply out of self-advocacy and wanting to improve
my health and functioning for purposes of thriving just wanted
to probe and inquire if perhaps humira might be a viable option
or possibility for my degenerative arthritis, as appears to help to
slow down the process and hit those specific acute and flaring areas;
again i have heard nothing back from her or your office. also too,
while taking care of my son today because he's sick, i get a mechanical
message for a mandated appointment which was made for me without
even my consent through central vermont; the complete and honest
truth e. and i are down one car at the present time due to a starter
problem and literally just had to have aaa over here the other day

just to start it up, but not safe being on the road until we get it fixed.
e. needs the other car because she works every day as a teacher at union
elementary so will not be able to make the appointment. again this
has developed a bit of an orwellian quality, as seems like there's this
protocol of which i am required to follow but not at all being included,
or being made a part of, or for that matter being provided any sort of
clarification about the status of things, even given disinformation (not
on purpose) by your secretaries speaking of a 'human error' saying
they've ameliorated the problem, but then h. saying never received
any fax and that she would call your practice and once again not
hearing back from anyone, yet appointment being made for me without
even asking. i saw my nurse yesterday (who does a really wonderful
and thorough job) and thanks for that, and she reported as well while
believe will be indicated in her notes that the wound has actually healed
quite well and there's practically very little left which presents with any
discoloration on my skin; a matter of fact the swelling has been reduced
and gone down profoundly in both legs, as have followed through
diligently with elevation, self-grooming, as well as being seen twice
a week by a pca in my home; again need to clarify, will not be able to
make appointment next week until we can get another car on the road,
and a. will confirm through her medical notes or progress notes leg
looks really good; sorry m. for a bit the rambling here, but taking care
of sick son right now and obviously feeling a bit frustrated and
disempowered. i think it is important every so often to be able to
express these things if in fact this is exactly what's happening and
am following through concisely, while doing a lot of the leg work
on my end. thanks and actually would love to maybe for purposes
of clarification just hear back from maybe your nurse or if time
affords you yourself over the phone, thank you kindly and take care

#21

You start to drink somewhere between
halloween and thanksgiving not necessarily
heavier but earlier due to the blue bleak over
cast weather when parts of your home start
shifting creaking in the change of seasons
and you gratefully welcome the phantoms
when all those triggers of living just makes
your life proportionately profoundly lonelier

        the grandfather clock comes alive
            along with scents of pork chops
                    & baked apples & wine

#22

We lie around seething (like some lion in captivity)
with our beer & tv surrounded by our knick-knacks &
tchotchkes our books & candles & checkers & firewood
& things we find self-soothing when the dogs start to die
down in the evening sometimes even just turn to the weather
& whiskey & for no apparent reason decide to just suddenly
strip off all our clothing & chop wood buck-naked with our
axe & balls swinging singing insanely grunting & huffing &
puffing in the middle of the deep dark wild howling midnight
mountain a short-order cook working at some bed & breakfast
for an abusive absentee innkeeper who lives down in florida
& shows absolutely no kindness or gratitude & just thrives
& loves to do her surprise visits & suddenly shows up like
some mean evil spinster after driving her man crazy &
everything which once ran like clockwork is thrown out
of sync having her employees bend over backwards & run
for cover & they all got that look on their face like they're
being held hostage & what was once autonomous & harmonious
all suddenly turns to instant conflict & power-struggles like
some real-life comedy of errors even been known to blackmail
& provide preferential treatment to the younger men for sexual
favors while people just pick up & leave & don't even give a
damn or care to collect their paycheck; hardworking loyal angels,
tearful hysterical head of housekeeping, front desk clerks, time
keepers, some young & single & pregnant, some abandoned
by their alcoholic boyfriends just to try to put food on the table
for their cherubic daughters & head back beatdown bleary-eyed
into the bleak beautiful mountains at dawn…

#23

When huck & jim awoke every morn
from the deep southern sun (squinting
already sweating with the stray seeping
scent of magnolia creeping through crepe
myrtle crickets still milling around) still
on-the-run from the slave master's gun
to go cross over that proverbial mason-
dixon line of freedom to live the so-called
life; adrenaline, blood pumping like the mighty
mississippi now that there is what you might
call having a sense of purpose and meaning

#24

In my opinion we all end up like ratso rizzo
never quite making it to the promised land
down in miami beach florida skull falling
on shoulders of best friend joe buck also
something of a failed hustler but a heart
of gold both former and future ghosts of
themselves in the back of some *greyhound*
bus right when the palm trees start to show up

#25

Dreams penetrate our consciousness like a rushing train
moving from city to city over the countryside to the sea

those geometric shapes and forms which seem to constantly
haunt us; a loneliness we can't escape from which won't let us
alone (and lose sleep over) even in our life when we try to move on

#26

It is the keen fear (all that angst and trepidation)
of the sudden loss of those archetypal shapes
and forms of object-permanence (real-life symbols)
developed in childhood and adolescence and the
life-transition of becoming an adult which brings
about a certain nihilistic, existential crisis of
sorts very rarely mentioned in those neat and
cerebral stages of mature human growth and
development, and only gets exacerbated by
a profound sense of (self-) denial (of severe
emotional loss along with perplexing desertion
and abandonment) with very little guidance and
support by guardians, who just seem totally self-
absorbed, unsympathetic, clueless and out-of-touch

Eventually those shapes and forms (i.e. a hometown,
a home, rooms in that home) concomitant with this
selfsame separation-anxiety develops something of
a 'foreign' quality, silent, strange, surreal and solitary

Proof:

Most memories take on configurations & forms
the morning mist of mountains, thick dense fogs
rolling in & out down long undulating roads of
the forest, the gleaming glow of crystal dewy
telephone wires, the treeline way up high
on the tippy-top of mountains, rising into
the radiant, rinsed-out rags of raggedy clouds
to know it's all really just some girl you once
loved, some ole, lonesome, broken down dog
plopped-down, taking his same spot, dozing-off
right in front of the fire, cranes coming in like foghorns

Proof:

The hog
in the fog
like the fog
horns at dawn

#27

Symbols and superstitions are far less symbolic and superstitious while interestingly at the same time simultaneously contain far more meaning than you may very well think...

#28

And so what if all we really are
is just some strange bizarre secret
at last finally penetrating the surface
suddenly discovered like the flutter
of autumnal leaves in the whispering
breeze way up above in the towering
teetering trees trembling in the holy
hush of some beautiful bleak calm
contemplative croaking lagoon each
season coming out just a little bit
different but just as solitary and
brilliant eavesdropping on evolution
and the murmur and movement
of mountains over the ages to
know sages are really just the
rumors of raconteurs passed
down from generation
to generation...

#29

The distance of the frozen over
lake from shoreline to shoreline
the distance of mist which blankets
the tippytop of sacred mountains
the distance of the boundaries of
reality & bounds of the imagination
the distance from star to star which
threads the limitless constellations
the distance between those
once loved & no longer around
the distance between ghosts & clowns
the distance of all things 'tween lost & found
the distance of all things broken & hollow
the distance of charm which is the leftover
remains of broken promises & betrayal
the distance of what we
once were & no longer are
the distance between what we once
believed in & lost somewhere down the road
the distance between coincidence & fate
which seems like all that's been bought & sold

#30

One wonders if there's some sort of mathematical proof
(of truths and non-truths) or time's table for our ultimate
redemption, and if it's already been proven we suffer on
a daily basis on an existential and zen-buddhist level maybe
instead just solely a list of similar-like elements and variables
(forms and images) or law of opposites, which will allow us
to finally reach that infamous fleeting solution of contentment

#31

On that day jesus walked on water one wonders
if he also wandered the swamps & lagoons
& haunted holy houses of the woods

At dusk what did he have for supper?
was it simply a feast of fish & spaghetti
squash & palm wine where the crickets
& fireflies suddenly just lived & died?

#32

Jigsaw puzzles on the wall in the hall
of that very quaint inn which wouldn't let
in mary the virgin *billions & billions served*

#33

One day there will be this ragamuffin thief kid
who will move the masses tap dance and play
harmonica in the cobblestone of new orleans

not run for one of those horrible corrupt infamous
powerful positions as leader of the free world when
kerosene lanterns come on and start to flicker at dusk

#34

We go all out
for those we love
i have even i swear
stolen and been sent
home in handcuffs.
with a slight grin
we declare our innocence
knowing deep down inside
never had a chance
(this was all a part
of the risk and romance)
and had absolutely
no one to fall back on
all those wild things
and shapes and forms
that were just out of reach
and what dreams
were not made of
we have a million
and one reasons
to steal and
get caught

#35

Always felt honored and flattered
by that good-natured thief just
as displaced, misunderstood
and underestimated as me
when she believed in me
and went all out for me
which is a real rarity
(these are the type
of people you never
quite forget) as most
of them just don't give
a damn and doubted and
questioned and seemed more
like something of an absurd
stingy interrogation. who was
it nietzsche said 'it's all about
the journey' and if that be the
case most of them just tourists
who come a dime a dozen who
don't see a thing around them

#36

You choose a dress for your manic kin
got no idea how much you love her
like the crumbs, like the seasons
wit, intuition (internal rhythms)
is a whole other kind of wisdom

#37

She put all her faith in me and for that
am eternally *indebted* thankful and sorry
and love her and guilty till the end of time

love hits you at the strangest of times
when you're just barely hanging on

#38

Looking back
at it all it all
was in all
those little nuances
those memories
those moments
you catching
her eye and
her catching
yours and
that spirit
meaning more
than i can even
begin to tell
that mad kiss
in the midst
of it all and
feeling all
the bullshit
evaporate
and dissolve
and fall down
all around
you realizing
absolutely
nothing matters
that it's all just
ephemeral
and permeable
everything instantly
magically forgotten
the past and the future
that it's all just an illusion
(what dreams are made of)
while the only thing that
stands is her and you
in the strange
obscure
beauty
of it all

#39

One becomes fluent in pillow talk
(she even told me it turned her on
which kind of turned me off as was
just acting natural and reciting my life
story of being a kid on the road with
absolutely no one to turn to and getting
it all off my chest) after all…after all the
bullshit & brainwash of how they thought
they could (p)reach me with a wink & nod

Proof:

When you find at this point of life
you're almost like one of those boys
in a group home who every time he gets
held or hugged freaks out and runs while
it wasn't until that crazy girl i met taught
me how to spoon and sleep and stay in
bed and when she took off and fled well
i won't tell you but did somehow make it
and find out in this existence you get strong
and grow by pretty much holding on and never
letting go no matter what doing the rope-a-dope

Proof:

Baby please bash my head in
so i can have feelings again
so i can remember to never
forget how much i always
loved you from begin end

Proof:

Has some madman shattered
this spare light bulb which
is the sadness of the soul
stars out tonight while
at least can sweep them
up and screw in a new one

Proof: how the heart & soul now composed
of the glow from old broken-up streetlights,
foghorns, and the distant echo of trains; the
faded beacon of those bus lights the only thing
in sight (a whole new insight) in that deep dark
desert night, one day colliding into the next, not
sure which one is which or where you were, and
this disoriented thought-pattern somehow making
your senses so much more keen and alert, solely
seeing the simple snake eye lights of some strange
midnight truck suddenly show up and coming at you
out of the night (at first unable to identify or define)
from the bleak endless manifest-destiny dust from
the west, escaping, stealing away from the east,
as nothing made you feel more alive and righteous
and put your mind at ease, while all things fleeting
seemed to release me from all those once absurd,
sedentary things (of so-called truths and meaning)
aimed to keep me down, something i suppose that
most likely stayed with me until the end of time…

Proof: those days literally feeling my heart
throbbing from my empty lonely hollow
soul suddenly seeing those holy deep
purplish low-hanging clouds show
up between the night and dawn
bleary-eyed through the bus
window taking *greyhounds*
from hell's kitchen all the way
to the real true-blue golden beacon
city on the hill suddenly materializing
in the distance awakening gleaming out
in the misty firmament of san francisco
crawling in a train from the insane stifling
heat of the big easy through thick dense
beat bogs and bayous back to my home
town in new york city from bleak motels
at the end of *burlington northern* boxcar
tracks literally roaming through the desert
of reno to try and land a job from gorgeous
first teenage love with eyes and spirit finally
wide open from the basement of her parent's
home in the snowy silent suburbs strolling miles
with real-life head in the clouds and everyone
still asleep in sleepy town somehow (and not
caring how) trying to find my way back home

Proof:

Our visions come when we are alone
taking those desperate journeys of
solitude and contemplation, based
on our own free will and volition
and see (know it all) in the sudden
moment through the window of the
rushing train, dusty bus, bleary-eyed
ferry, taking off and arriving on some
plane in some foreign land (which does
not seem 'foreign' at all) no longer
a stranger, but feeling completely
at home, comfortable in our own skin
with those people and things we have
never known (but somehow have made
some sort of past metaphysical connection)
our heart and soul full of keen, palpable spirit
receptive and open; a good fugitive on-the-run
spiritually at one, far away from that culture
and environment, which has been so absurdly
obscurely forced on us vaguely labled as home

Proof:

There are still some great thriving communities
that fine fried chicken joint with cottage fries
right off prospect park in brooklyn you'd
pick up after a long anonymous summer's
day wandering contented being absolutely
nowhere yet still feeling very much a part
of (in a constant fleeting state of flux);
a stranger on the outskirts drifting home
home at dusk when the foghorns came
down and clotheslines went up…

Proof:

They waste saints in amerika until you're so damn drained
after working the graveyard hustling a cab in new york city
standing all alone stoned wasted & wired from exhaustion
at 5 in the morn on the platform in herald square for a train
that'll never come to the last stop on stillwell avenue coney
island with the blaring blinding sun coming up over the
washed-out neon brokedown rickety-rackety *cyclone*
rollercoaster staggering off like some soul survivor
picking up your bag of fruit & nuts & tall can of beer
& paper to get the scores from the night before hearing
the surreal waves pound the shore which become
that much more palpable to the senses due to all the
chaos and madness from the night before but strangely
enough although keen and even serene really with no
feeling at all disassociating (not really caring mattering
at all to make sense of it all knowing really nothing to
make sense of) wandering home with the stray dogs

Proof:

How the sun slightly skimming
off the ledge of pigeons some
where around lunch hour at
12:36 during the christmas
season always kept you
grounded always kept
you company keeping
you from feeling lonely
during your swingshift
working as a front desk
clerk at *the times square hotel*
right 'round the corner from
that corner hell's kitchen bar
room specializing in highballs
and a shoot-out each and every
evening increasing its turnover rate
finding it difficult to keep bartenders

postal police making their rounds...

Proof:

Why not ever a picture of
the burntdown roller disco
the skate key in the bronx
for holiday cards as in my
estimation evokes emotions
both intuitive and universal
of our time here on earth…

Proof:

Still have that crazy-like fantasy-dream of driving
some ice cream truck all the way cross-country
and to make my gas money sell these popsicles
to half-crazed hysterical kids who come racing
hollering wailing trotting toot-tooting towards
my open welcoming window for their vanilla
and fudge push-up pops and bomb pops
and take routes never took before this time
through old fugitive montana partners on
the run from the res. for no other reason
but to be on-the-run through ole radiant
ramshackle cities always seeming to just
be teetering on the brink on top of turn
of the century hills in holy alleys and
ol' haunted victorians of st. paul minnesota
that lost woebegone town where the clothes
still hang upside down and low down on the
clothesline coming out of kansas city finally
at last reaching no man's land in the land of
milk & honey gorges & canyons of forgotten
idaho where i used to truly be on my own in
my early twenties and knew all the truckstops
with the best biscuits & gravy and waitresses
who treated me like royalty some i swear who
even took me in so nice and sweet and moments
like that i'll always remember and never forget
and guess will just rest in some little carved-out
berth set right behind the driver's seat like when
i used to pack a pistol beneath the hot spring
mountains of lumberjack lost midnight train
yards of portland, oregon reciting the "i'm a
scared! i'm a scared!" holy mantra blues beneath
the solitude of the moon and when they ask me
why i'm doing this all i mean what's it all for
will simply provide no real plausible answer
like some buddha bodisattva soldier returning
home from war just wanting to be left alone
drained jesus forrest gump after he finally
stopped running after years and years of
being on the road and that there in having

no particular political purpose or cause
will be the most profound thing i can
possibly come up with and think of

Proof:

Why
would
anyone
attend
a lecture
at the end
of the world
at some hole
in the wall
holiday inn
"free hbo"
wond'ring
wha duh
ya want
with a
hobo
while
imagine
have to
be as
lost as
a drunk
in sales
man as
the sex
pistols
who
got
booked
gigs
in one
of those
one horse
town bar
& lounges
in the
deep
south
at the
end

of
the
70's
when
they
uttered
that in
famous
phrase–
"ever feel
like you
been
cheated?"

Proof: language when deconstruct
its linguistic patterns subliminally
subconsciously and spiritually
becomes very closely similar
to a cross between fate and
coincidence without consciously
being aware of it— my bucket list
(although always hated such
obvious contrived expressions)
would be vegas, already lived
in reno at the end of the universe
madrid, already been to valencia
& barcelona, cordoba & grenada
already done costa del sol & sevilla
the andes mountains mostly traveled
mostly most of south central america
going down to downtown florence
already all over italy & sicily
& got some family i believe
in the fashion industry who
moved from milan to rome
who's got a boat which can
take us out to the coast
to that remote island
in the middle of the
mediterannean
where's that?
malta? corsica?
where napolean
got his start
grew up
& was born
& suppose last but
not least scandinavia
what are they? norway
finland & sweden?
always loved
ingmar bergman

Proof:

Scenes and things that effect us most
freud spoke about it in his 'wit and its
relation to the unconscious' for me it's
sentimental scenes from bergman movies
from "the graduate" and "midnight cowboy"
when guidry struck out 19 in 77 and chris
chambliss hit his infamous homer in the
pennant not so much walking down the aisle
but her accepting my offer when least expected it

Proof: recollection suddenly hearing
"alice in chains unplugged" while
over in sicilia when those gigolos
tried to hustle me on the beach
which was cool but just never
ever really into...more into
the mythological goddesses
strolling on the promenade
always just out of reach
poverty-stricken studs
with rich daughters
on the back of their
vespas buzzing uphill
to the disco at dusk…

Proof:

Maybe there's something
wrong with me i don't think
but always liked those cute girls
with mad moxie who might put
on their plum-wine nail polish
and blow their hair while sitting
up on top the bathroom sink
in the morning driving their
boyfriends crazy (who
the mothers hate and
sons fall in love with
following in their
footsteps) while
she tells off her boss
in public cause just
sick of their shit
and injustices and
in transition taking
shots at polish diners
jotting down poems in
notebooks looking out
over the park at all the
madness of humanity

Proof:

What a weird and wild and obvious and mean
and malicious concept and saying to get "thrown
out" i mean to get thrown out by your girlfriend
and what exactly would be involved with that
getting thrown out and what are the words that
would be said while being thrown out and is there
any back and forth like you never really loved me
or please you know i didn't mean any of those things
or do you just finally paradoxically accept it and feel
something of a sense of relief and do you actually sigh
a sigh of relief and what do you think you might put in
that infamous duffel bag anything from the refrigerator
bagels and cream cheese and the wine which has been
fermenting like moonshine hotdogs and sauerkraut
tv dinners and frozen orange juice the short stories
by fyodor dostoevsky and all of proust you've been
meaning to get to your guitar and postcards and
shoelaces and would you also put in those actual
pictures of old girlfriends some nude and some just
of seduction and tube socks and high top sneakers
and when you get thrown out where do you head
to first the y or some pal in the upper west side or ask
your sister for a couple weeks in brooklyn or supervisor
from the mental health clinic or the girlfriend before this
one where you had a great sexual intimate relationship and
opened her up and think she should be grateful and thank
full enough and never got full closure and should let you
back in after you get thrown out for some of the stupidest
shit while just a real bad mood you were both in that
morning and things didn't go exactly as planned

Proof:

It's crazy but when they drive you crazy
you literally pick up and leave pack up
your bags with spinoza & nietzsche
copy of a dsm for mood & personality
& richie rich & archie and head down
to costa rica the region right on the border
of panama and take a tiny hut on a black
sand beach hearing a tree frog chirping
the whole time hidden somewhere up
in the bamboo beams and just like every
thing else having to do with reality and
being have to learn to adapt and accept
it and get used to it; in the morning swipe
a couple bananas from a banana tree right
outside my shutters and stroll down a long
sandy street into town where at the same time
i see happy smiling and laughing poor school
girls in their parochial school dresses peddling
their bikes to class as you trample all day
on the shore along the rainforest and once
literally get stuck for a moment i swear in
quicksand get myself out and spend the rest
of my days contemplating and getting my head
straight (on one of those river rafts seeing white
monkeys swinging from the trees water hippos
and jesus christ lizards skimming on the seas)
discovering the most dangerous species are not
necessarily the vultures just sitting and hanging
out harmlessly hunched way up on the tops of
palm trees in the morning but the human beast

Proof:

The hx of man corrupts practically everything
the docks, the unions, sports, politics, religion,
the seas rising; eventually is it just gonna be
another tragic noah catastrophe? these days
all you see on your tv is one computer-generated
archetype fighting another, as you end up having
no sympathy for any of the characters; how we
so easily forget how all great greek mythology
(its tragedies, its comedies) even ancient egypt
began from some fertile land and culture
and civilization of purpose and meaning

in the end like some brilliant nightmarish
dream are all we gonna see glowing are
the pyramids or mcdonald's golden arches
waking up in the morning at *the nile condominiums*
with signs just staked up reading "under new management?"

Proof:

How about a dream where the signs point everywhere?
to the safari. to the refreshments. to the entertainment.
to the lavatory. and we go absolutely nowhere realizing
our lives are so pathetically and completely incomplete.
and not sure if this is a dream or nightmare like some
grand museum for the end of the world. how there's
such a fine line and not really much of a difference
between fate and coincidence or making it. you bump
into old acquaintances who seem more like strangers.
everyone is a tourist who appears in a state of mourning
even the cute coquettish girls and not sure who is doing
the seducing nor if any of that would even matter while
all you dream about is just getting home to your wife
and kids in this foreign land of the eternally absurd.
you will take a transfer to get you there because
you are streetwise and been practically everywhere
and just stand in a dark bathroom breathing aloud
trying to get this all out of your head. there's some
thing to be said about turning that proverb on its head
and forgetting and forgiving yourself. one should not
always be so thoughtful. one should not always care

Proof:

After the senseless sacrifice and slaughter
at the end of the war an award ceremony
thrown with blaring flashbulbs going off.
the stands stand empty and bare where
both winners and losers are forced to
go through the ritual of kneeling and
kissing the queen's hand. a gigantic
sized check is presented by the sponsor
from some sort of foreign oil conglomerate
and when they exit the arena they're followed
by the prince and princess, alcoholic lounge
act, the stand-up comedian still cracking
one-liners and the children of the village
who are supposed to represent something
idealistic like the future. on a big beat-up
screen is a ridiculous image of the dictator
king with a killer smile like a porn star in
paradise or machiavellian pedophile, while
in the corridor old timers mill around like
zombies with gambling problems, as just
outside the coliseum where they used to
house slaughterhouses and whorehouses
they've all been converted into climate-
controlled condominiums conveniently located
with easy access to the mall made for practically
every occasion and population during the life-cycle
from the toddler to the teenage slut daughter
to the greaser to the miserable housewives who
feel ignored by husbands no longer paying attention
to them and passive-aggressively spending all their
money cashing out their credit cards to retirees like
old fishermen just sitting drained at some fountain
of youth where they toss in those coins for wishes
for the future looking like they finally have a little
downtime with their nagging wives shopping
in the dollar stores. outside down the perfectly
pristine boulevard you see a massive billboard
rising to the clouds with a huge higher than
holy glossy photo of the news team like false
gods with insincere smiles simply reminding

us they're the team to trust and you think if
they are you got absolutely no one and just
fantasize about that cute anchorwoman just
sitting on your lap during the holiday season

Proof: sometimes you just get
so damn lonely you don't
even know you're lonely
worst thing about being
lonely just being lonely
who came up with that one
'flying the friendly skies'
as the best part for me
always like arriving at
charles de gualle and
asking the dwarf cab
driver to take me to
my b & b in monmartre
and him cranking on french
french rap literally snapping
fingers barreling past le tour
d'eiffel through winding
cobblestone taking off
a couple weeks later in
the early morning from le
gare de lyon and suddenly
seeing on the tgv that whole
swath of the mediterannean
showing up around the bend
as if miraculously sprouting
from the sea literally running
for the ferry after crossing
border from france to italy
into the industrial city
of milan and the ferries
simply reading at dawn
w. africa/napoli arriving
the next morning after
a day out at sea with
strange slapstick
vaudeville and
miserable poor
aristocrats in foreign
languages through
the thick mists
while suddenly

exists like the lost island
of atlantis in sicily bleary
eyed taking the taxi through
decadent palm trees to palermo
glowing holy sacred in the
cradle of mafia mountains
cars set on fire while bright
eyed brides and grooms
wander down cobblestone
alleys to the sea getting off
the trains and innocently
looking for a taxi in venice
and them all just being
speedboats racing through
the ancient lagoon of peach
and periwinkle pastel shutters
to your long-lost destination
long train ride from venice
to lake lugana crazy cabins
flocks of sheep teetering
way up high in the clouds
of swiss alps on the border
of italy and switzerland
getting out of the train
station smacked instantly
with the aromatic heat
of sweltering fragrant
orange orchards they
make marmalade
out of in sevilla
into the jewish quarter
of verdant catacombs
and courtyards and
gypsies seeing in
the distance in greece
skeleton bones of the
acropolis show up in
the contemporary slums
and ruins of athens early morn
racing towards the agean with
your loved one on your honey
moon and nodding-out at stray

dog cafes waiting for your boat
once more heading way out to
the mythological whitewashed
cliffs of santorini in the off-season
while would it be at all absurd or
crazy to say cause 'in a certain place'
never once worrying about your future

Proof:

Civilization in ol' time europa is the spirit
of street urchins in the sandlot of the slums
& wannabe old money aristocrats strolling
past the opera house & ancient cathedral
on the sea at dusk; priests & gigolos & widows
with glimmering svelte bottles in shop windows
of limon liqueur from the orchards in the mountains
the last of merchants sweeping up his sidewalk; your
rucksack full of rolls of film waiting to get developed
still full of maps & sand your new lover laughs & cleans out

Proof: it's interesting not really
i've read all poetry and philosophy
from top to bottom from the beginning
to the end of time all those french and
russian and greek classics all books
of the dead and manuals and guides
for domestic and wild animals statistics
and criteria for psychological disorders
but the one thing that always hits me
and moves me the most is a simple
foreign film which usually takes place
somewhere in the backstreets of paris
a love story or interlude and moment in
time between some man and woman facing
all the challenges and obstacles of life and
their self-destructive personality traits and
characteristics until you realize the only
thing that really matters is true romance
as just gets you up from your chair to
manage to move on just a couple more
days in this absurd rotten existence we
ridiculously refer to as our time on earth

Proof: has anyone ever been a widower of thy own
self requiring a rebirth practically on a daily basis
like a brand new pot of coffee, *captain crunch*
a mistress and masturbation? i think i'll find
i'm finally happy when they finally overthrow
the government and everyone and all sides
and stations and parties just shut the fuck
up, while all i hear is the silence of the snow
of the season, her beating heart, and beat of
the brook through bulletproof window. why
did sartre ask such inane questions like prove
that you exist as think it'd be so much more germane
and relevant in questioning everything and everyone
around him. the hypocrites never once ever sent me
a card, like absurdly seeming to be having to take a
make-up exam based on my own guilt and conflict
and something i was sincerely never ever really that
interested in in the first place or a part of, like some
mandated cruise i am forced to go on (with strangers
i loathe and have absolutely no respect for) to prove
my commitment; in love and belief in the whole
concept, and decide instead to just lock myself
up in the cabin the whole time, while so much
more in touch with my senses and stray scents
of the sea seeping through my porthole (based
on real-life experience of being a scorned lover
and fugitive of sorts) as feel like i get so much
more and they arrest me at the next port based
on some sort of mix-up or mistaken identity.
bureaucracy, interrogation(s), paranoia
petty rules and regulations are all pathetic
and ridiculous hypocrisies and contradictions
of human nature (the humorless human creature).
the puppeteers, lounge singers, and comedians
are all on strike and i am required myself and
they won't tell me why. when i finally make
it back home a broken, complete man, it will
be by the light of day, enlightened, enraptured
in the land of the blind by those who ironically
went out of their way to try and ostracize and
ignore and turn their back on me in the first

place, while i was raised the right way, and
all i knew was to try and try till my dying day

Proof: scenes from the ventriloquist convention

I don't know— i'm probably wrong but back in the day
cooperatives seemed more like a bunch of avant-garde
writers and artists perhaps getting together in the pubs
of paris like gertrude stein and hemingway and picasso
all literal starving artists but had so much to contribute
and offer and now just feels like a clique of crunchy
pseudo-intellectual liberals who make it very clear
how you cannot be a part of their club (more like
some coop board of rich daughters who all for
style and attitude prefer lopsided floorboards
and clawfoot tubs) and awfully exclusive and
all about who you know and giving out to each
other awards and think it's cool to claim brooklyn
as their own but there's nothing further from the truth
while those who can just afford to buy their own brown
stones or converted lofts and condos, and only a couple
of stops on the subway to wallstreet and tribeca and soho
and seem more like these pathetic, politically-correct, spoiled,
wannabe, quasi-diverse yuppies with suburban souls— shoot
i think i'd actually even prefer to become a member of some
country club as almost feels more genuine in their targeted
goal of money-grubbing and make no bones about it while
be great fodder for satire…

Proof: scenes from the scream

Superintendent of schools sent out one of those group e-mails
that they are looking for a new principle for our school district.
could you imagine having spent a whole adolescence in detention
eventually just sitting there at a big idiot desk of administration
(like some guilty kid with a great big grin getting them all back
for doubting me now surrounded by my subordinates i can't stand
for respecting me) a name plate right in front of me which just
reads "principle" polished glowing just sitting there like some
snickering slapstick vaudeville comedian having to get out
the last of his last-ditch punchlines in the prime of his life
while the theater emptied-out a long time ago…

I thought this was supposed to be
one of those good school systems?

Proof: scenes from the pharmaceutical convention

At my power point presentation it would just be held in
one of those awful conference rooms like at some *holiday
inn* up in the industrial hills with just a pointer and projector
and not believing in anything politically-correct would take
one of those mandated kiss asses and social climbers right
in front of the symposium and whack the hell out of them
right on the bottom of their tuckis male and female alike
dickensian-style until i get all possible information out
of them and then deconstruct and debate all possible
hypothesis and conceptual ideas in a rather dramatic
hissy/trionic manner as always been a big believer in
getting so much more out of the individual by being
interactive with a control group and experimental
group and be nun of those idiot multiple choice tests
you are required to pass which provide you absolutely
no real knowledge or gets you anywhere in the real
world as just simply a baseline study for each person
to reach their targeted potential and with pain/pleasure
dried-up crocodile tears all creep out much better men
women and organisms to the morning smokestacks mixing
with the rising sun like one of those warm cheese danishes

Proof:

What would it be like to be famous?
imagine it'd be a lot like that ground
hog coming out of his hole on a daily basis
surrounded by those moles in top hats and tuxedos
being cheered on for simply seeing his own shadow

Proof:

Has anyone ever thought to play *batman* backwards
and have him & the boy wonder sliding up the batpole
in reverse right into the bruce wayne manor (alfred
on their shoulder) and all those things which led up
to the crisis which in my opinion is just the humdrum
monotonous routines & rituals of our everyday reality
& existence all that nihilism which feeds our nightmares
everyone at the dinner party & reunion & funeral seem
to be acting the exact same way trying to make the exact
same impression (playing these roles with no soul of self-
promotion) and you don't see the point and make no effort
while can't seem to make a connection as just think about
what you should get at that delicatessen out in brooklyn
avoiding that whole review session of gossip & rumors

drifting home content in the throng of churchbells & foghorns

Proof:

If it's all about timing
i must be waiting eternally
on some corner for a bus
that will never show...

Proof:

What if i died several years ago
and simply just a ghost of my former self
which in fact turns out a far better version?

Proof:

Life and death simply bureaucratic…

Proof:

Self-fulfilling prophecy is that line of rockettes
kicking up their legs falling over the precipice

Proof:

A whole revolution (overthrow of a government) recorded on a tourist's smartphone; if we lose the recording or hopefully the tourist did it ever go down?

Proof:

The boy on the moon
is just as lonely as you
eating milk & cereal
looking down on you

Proof:

Sometimes it feels like we're just this grand magic trick unaware of our secrets but if we dig just a little bit deeper…

Proof:

"No more or no less"
damn when you think
about it isn't that like
one of the greatest
buddhist statements?

Proof:

Did gertrude ever order in?

Proof:

A strange thing to me but often in the city
i seemed to feel more the seasons— maybe
had something to do a little with melancholy
and being solitary and reflective and the senses
and feeling all those elements penetrate my being

Proof:

When a new day shows up
and the mountains & lakes
light up it's like some magical
monochromatic coloring book
somewhere between the silent
night & holy dawn; you shake
off the phantoms forced
to become a former
ghost of yourself

Proof:

We barely survive suburbia
like some existential surreal
prison sentence we're not
even aware we're serving

Proof:

Looking back, those pals of mine pretty good
down-to-earth guys who started self-medicating
at pretty young ages when their parents went away
to their second home in the berkshires; little bits
of hash wrapped up in tinfoil ending up getting
like straight a's going to ivy league colleges

Proof:

It's really hard to take any sort of advice
from most guys cause there's always some
element & dynamic of jealousy & envy involved

do they still have ferries going out to tunisia?

Proof:

I like watching the world news
and whenever they have some
sort of revolution or uprising
showing some poor stray dog
curiously sniffing the riot squad
perhaps over their in lesbo, greece
with the hootie rebels or the muslims
and hindus and when i see the smoke
and stones flying find i can always relate
so much more and feel sympathy for just
that simple stray dog sniffing the toy soldiers

hey did you know there's a mayor
for each and every arrondisement?

Proof:

The one thing you pick up when watching
the news is that man is just simply so fucked-up
and corrupt from top to bottom from the gardener
to the fisherman to the street sweeper to publishing
to advertising to the construction workers putting
up skyscrapers to the wallstreeters to politicians to
the prime minister to the president to police and peasants
going back and forth in a real-life power-struggle between
throwing stones and returning tear gas canisters with those
constantly infringing on each others borders and launching
missiles and going into instant denial while it just becomes
he-said she-said by a bunch of diplomatic devil compulsive
liars to the embalmers to the professional mourners; who was
it think it was ralph kramden played by the late-great great one jackie
gleason when he declared 'you're gonna meet the exact same people
on the way up as you do on your way down' until you just find out
hx of culture & civilization is pretty much simply a repeat episode

Proof:

The tourist appears to always obsessively be searching for something (in the most safe and secure, uncreative and conformist of ways) while not by coincidence, paradoxically, once he gets there, doesn't know exactly what he's seeing, or even for that matter, 'what to make of it' due to his intrinsically impulsive and judgmental nature (so self-absorbed and insecure ironically alienating 'the natives' and treating them something like slaves there to just 'serve them') which appears representative to the psychodynamic and phenomenon of human nature and the human condition, as well as all the hypocrisies and injustices of the original 'class' struggle and caste system

Proof:

War & westerns & the weather & wrestling
a genre which has lasted forever in america
jingles for fast food, endless sirloin, seafood
psycho/tropics & farm-o-pseudo-calls that'll
save you & cure the blues & make you—
'the leisure class' to a certain extent
still exists in the form of pristine and
placid, artificial, insular suburbia with
its materialistic items and status symbols
the personification and main component
for proof of self-worth and what it means
to be "a success" in the free-enterprise,
capitalistic and very competitive, cut-throat
democratic system; the term 'love thy neighbor'
an irrelevant and antiquated expression due to the
basic rude vulgar nature of man, while used purely
for purposes of self-interest and to take advantage
which more times than not manifests itself in all those
natural, primal instincts full of hypocrisies and contradictions
and becomes so much a part of and ingrained and hardwired
in man's demeanor, character, and behavior (eventually on
the most absurd and surreal of levels) not even aware of it

Monster becomes a martyr and back again
and backs his ship into the driveway…

Proof:

Mankind (neither men nor kind that infamous kind
of biblical neighbor) more often than not will play
the real-life role of protagonist or provocateur trying
to play you out (like some classic shakespeare villain)
as if you were the one who started it at being impulsive
and hostile when all you ever were doing was minding
your own and simply defending your right to function
and thrive (the amount of time they invest and life they
waste with their petty mind games) as literally are forced
to protect your dignity and self-respect and at times even
due to their selfish aggressive and barbaric behavior have
to prove that there will be natural consequences to get them
to stop and then will almost always follow the behavioral
pattern of playing possum with their phony privileged and
entitled character all of a sudden not so complacent and arrogant

Proof:

Those of mediocrity will constantly drag you into their mediocrity like an alcoholic always trying to make you the cause to their problems

Proof:

Following politics or even for that matter taking it seriously
would be like a ball team you've always loved since you
were a kid, but know they'll always find some way of
doing some really dumb shit and blowing it, breaking
your heart and letting you down, asking that rather
ironic question of what did i do to deserve this?

Proof:

People don't exactly keep their word...
which develops something of an absurd
quality and think the more sincere and
earnest they sound the more down to
earth and people of truth and integrity
they are but there can be nothing further
from the truth (with this faulty baseline)
having everyone even themselves conned

Proof:

What is it? growing up was always some element of manipulation,
taken advantage, emotional blackmail, and some quasi-moral
and ethical ultimatum (which always left you more confused
and conflicted, while feeling constantly guilty and hostile)
looking back you really were like some wild seething animal
in a cage with a primal, but also spiritual need to escape,
do something crazy, and even act-out (which was not
necessarily a bad thing but almost inevitable) to establish
an identity and curiously explore all those things of existence
and reality (without even being aware of it of similar-like bullshit
domination and authority) and if you got into a little trouble so be
it (all good and no problem) while all those schmucks who over-
therapeutized or used and abused their power with sweeping and
obvious, cliché, clinical terms wanted to steal from them as well

Proof:

All those things you think are making you depressed
may in fact have absolutely nothing to do with it but
more so all those obvious things or rather obvious
people whose obvious offers and promises and
traits and characteristics (you pretty much know
from the start) just keep on repeating themselves
over and over and over again but what eventually
gives you wisdom from the very beginning is to
not proactively engage in these types of relations
as you can see (read and identity) all the repeated
behavioral patterns from previous past experiences

Proof:

All those things which haunt us at one point of our life
once held great, sentimental meaning and now takes on
the form of a whole other spiritual, keen, perceptive energy
and like the dynamic and process of osmosis, penetrates
that very damaged and porous, fragile membrane to the
core of our being; ghosts become the mythical manifestation
(in form and function) of the transformation between these
dueling states of reality (a mania of hallucinatory agitation
and anxiety) between trauma and drama, a sense of belonging
and alienation, meaning and purpose and loss of innocence
the elements and delicate details of the wild, fluctuating
seasons, the windy slamming of phantom shutters, creaking
of furniture & opening & shutting of natural fissures, spirit
of the inside/outside human anatomy, clinging, clattering
changing thought patterns & moods & behavior & reality

Proof:

They remain stuck to their smartphones
and don't see a thing around them.
am i the only one who seems to notice
the absurd irony of this satirical culture?

you pass from country to country
and see all of idiot pristine cul-de-sac
suburbia along the side of the highway
like a blueprint for empty reality with
out ever any single person out there

the border patrol always love to harass me
and interrogate me for at least 15 minutes
(what a strange abusive form of 'fame')
with questions that make absolutely no sense
at all and circumlocutious and irrelevant but when
see can't rattle me (as simply got used to these types
of things a long time ago) get hostile and frustrated
and upon leaving them try to start speaking to me
in a threatening manner almost as if giving me a
warning, as didactically, sardonically played them
out at their own game and start to become defensive
for being offensive (like control freaks who could not
quite exert their authority); at that point make it very
clear by my tone of voice not to cross that boundary
and need to watch their mouth and manners and the
sexless border agent almost acts shocked (that it's
not some sort of honor and no longer willing to
play that role) like a badboy coming back at her

when my wife gets heated when we get into canada
i tell her don't sweat them they're trying their best
and they're just confused with their identity
and think they're making an honest living

(there are windmills in filthy fields of corn
next to rows of motels and strip clubs and
feels like some sort of postmodern wasteland)

in the back of my head having been married
for some time now actually think the guard
was kind of cute in her uniform and have
the fantasy of giving her our hotel and
room number for a menage-a-trois
if wants to interrogate me anymore
while looks like she has not had a
substantial relationship in so long

her/ego could never be one of those
happy people posing in a photo
matter of fact those happy people
could never be happy people posing
in a photo hitherto why i'll never be
a happy person posing in a photo…

Proof:

The amount of time genet spent in jail
before jean-paul sartre bailed him out
believing he really had something of
substance to offer the public and culture

When wittgenstein came to bertrand russell inquiring
if he should be a philosopher or take up the life of
an inventor russell asked him to write just one line
and knew right there and then what his calling was

Nietzsche picked up the philosophical style of aphorisms
mostly in "beyond good and evil" due to his poor health
while only able to write for a certain amount of time in one
sitting apparently quite fond of la rochefoucald's "maxims"

When baudelaire's "le fleur de mal" got translated
into english he cleverly commented i hope we can
find a good translator to translate it back into french

Rimbaud the infamous boy genius french poet
(pretty much responsible for the symbolist movement)
when dying of syphilis his sister at the end of his life
was by his bedside trying to nurse him back to health

Kafka grew up with an abusive domineering father
which was a theme that influenced and ran through
a majority of his novels and upon his death requested
to an acquaintance that they should never ever be put
out to the public (perhaps due to his own self-image
of self-loathing and that of being kafkaesque) while
this was the one time that she over rode his request

Edgar allen poe lived a similar adolescence
of damage and desertion and abandonment
and wrote on similar tormented subject matters
in macabre fashion, while ironically developed
very much the same sort of 'existential' reputation

Tesla found on the steps of the ny public library
when they were giving out the awards for electricity

#40

Confidence is all that shit that kills you in the end
cause realize in the beginning was all built on illusion

*from a contrary point of view always had
  something of a sixth sense, yet ironically
  always ended up in the negative numbers

*people have a tendency to look too deeply
  into the most shallow of things; likewise, ironically
  too shallow with things that hold the most meaning

*treat you like a thief
  & accuse you of things
  you're not even guilty
  matter of fact quite the
  opposite & got all their
  info from jealous devils
  & been through it all
  & never had a mean
  bone in your body & give
  them the food off your plate
  & shirt straight off your back
  what gave all shakespeare's
  saints sudden heart attacks

*always felt so much more comfortable and satisfied
  in being on the outside, as once you got inside, they
  constantly felt like the kind who just never really
  paid their dues, and so much more casual and
  natural with their rationalizing and lies

*whenever i see people being real competitive
  they always look so pathetic like 'runner-
  ups' who lost the contest a long time ago

*as a child, were such wild and happy exhibitionists
  of the good kind, then the blinds just started closing
  for reasons i can't quite put my finger on it...

*crow streaks across purple
morning mist of mountains
i must still somehow exist

*a sunlit window
in raining woods

*one should write haiku
about the tree frogs
after the thunder

*slope of mountains like sagging
clotheslines in the purple dusk

#41

When and if we have an intimate affair
it's like a real-life game of truth or dare

grasping at a spirit we lost
somewhere down the road
and hope one day to repair
and even heal the despair

#42

It felt like i had been
in the streets for
a million years
and right after
we got engaged
and moved out
to providence
rhode island
to a place where
finally nobody
knew us (she
hadn't moved
up there yet
both already
set up for jobs
as social workers
out in the old ramshackle
cobblestone of newport)
while used to spend my days
killing time contemplating
just wandering around
the *providence place mall*
as felt comforting like some
sort of shelter or sanctuary
where i belonged or reborn
(should have an epic poem
where they record the feelings
and emotions of convicts right after
they get out of jail) and after popping
my head into all those *bed bath &
beyond* stores and all those light
classical masterpieces sunk into
my soul headed back home right
around sundown following all those
stray rivers over the fishermen bridges
to our nice little postage stamp lawn and
cape across from the vfw on the narranganset
bay going down with the bleak peaceful day
(cups of pumpkin coffee keeping me going)

falling asleep with the church bells and
foghorns on the mattress on the floor

#43

Most of my dreams seem to revolve
around the theme of some best friend
buddy from childhood who lived next
door running away with his grownup
daughters with luggage always ready
never taking off; your parents staying
at the sprawling, luxurious hotel with
the sun-lit revolving doors, visiting
you on the weekend at the prison
specializing in fugitives, constantly
guilty, confused, conflicted from
absentee manipulative father figurers
who care more about alumni dinners

you turn towards older women…

#44

At the bed & breakfast junkie brothers
beat-up each other for their mother's
possessions who presents as something
of a priceless, shattered widow, who
takes all her desertions out on the young
honeymooners with a whole life ahead
of them, having to escape and sneak
out of miniature midnight windows

#45

If only dreams really
was life turned inside
out and thus wake up
a new man with the
world off your shoulders

i tell you though there's a spirit…

#46

I got no one left to share my
schubert & schostakovich with

bach's 3 violins…

#47

Remember that game pick-up sticks
always so fun to play on a rainy
day when you just had nothing
else to do nothing left to say

Life seemed to get
so complicated after that
like kids playing with matches

#48

I think after we're done with the impeachment inquiry
of this madman psychopath, they should do one for the
vice president mike pence, the great evangelical christian
to prove if he's still alive looking like some soulless statue
in a wax museum, and every other senator who just stood idly
blindly by while this megalomaniac reality show star took over
the world. into the three amigos who look more like the three
stooges without the humor. into pompeo and our great attorney
general who seem to incriminate themselves every time they go
on such *hummanahummanahhummana* talk shows like "good
morning america." into kellyanne conway and her mixed-up
message marriage. into mitch mcconnell if in fact he is the
actual white devil. into rudolph goulioni who looks like some
mr. potato head count dracula or corrupt half-crazed accountant
with insomnia. into lindsay graham the higher-than-holy
hypocrite who changes his allegiance on a daily basis. into
that senator kennedy down in louisiana and how dare he
take on the family name of the ones in hyannisport. into
the wicked regeneration/reincarnation of that pedophile
circus-cowboy roy moore down in sweet home alabama
and that gomer pile sheriff in arizona who picks up soulful
softspoken hardworking migrants like picking cotton. into
every last single one of them in those areas and swaths they
supposedly call the bible belt the great state of texas the
heartland the rust belt and those last couple of vital swing
states which could all do for a whole heck of a lot more
swinging and if in fact we are really this great democracy
and beacon on the hill still engaged in the great political
experiment instead of the voter booth with the man behind
the curtain charging volts and bolts of electricity into them
for the death penalty demanding transparency should wire
and hook them all up to *life support* on prime time tv for
a whole battery of question answers of lie detecting with
an overhead projector beaming the red white and blue
stripes tape recording of the national anthem all those
brave bombastic bombs blasting off in the background
violent gunshots and superimposed studs cool and casual
strolling from fireball explosions from action-adventure
commercials for the number #1 movie in bullying believe it
or not everything-must-go white bred make america great again

AP: Left Out Clause From Constitution Now Modern-Day Manifesto

And so nowadays we literally have our real-life atticus finch mr. smith going to washington, arguing their case for the american people and inquiring and imploring, like some old blues gospel, negro spiritual– "can i get a witness?" in front of this higher-than-holy, might-over-right, machiavellian senate, who presents as this soulless, stubborn, surreal parable to that proverb 'ignorance is bliss' and honestly what is going to be written in the history books and told to our kids several decades later when we had all this information and data and proof and piles of evidence and simply were told were not allowed to use it, using the same line of communication and chain of command from an abusive commander-in-chief to his present day sycophants doing his bidding (ironically the exact same line of communication, blackmail, and extortion) of what he's originally being prosecuted for and how can we in any way, shape or form in good conscience explain and justify how we are in any way different than any other third world government, communist regime, or even for that matter, military dictatorship, and isn't this exactly what they warned us against and everything we fought so hard for in order to gain our freedom in this great democratic experiment when we drafted the original constitution and even declaration of independence where we have a modern-day monarch who is following all the exact behavioral and political and social-cultural patterns from recent history of fascism, trying to take over and control the media, all means of communication, manipulating and brainwashing the masses and status-quo, so i guess it just goes to show all we are simply asking is "can i get witness?" and wondering if in fact with this great beacon on the hill if those lights are still on, working, and in operation?

Addendum:

I. The Real Articles

I think the thing that bothers me the most
about this whole impeachment thing, like
asking the existential question did the dems
sell the case (or seal the deal) to the american
people are they're all a bunch of fucken
idiots who voted him in in the first place
(and all they just seem to care about is
the state of the economy) like what
else needs to be proven and seen?
robbing a liquor store at gunpoint
on america's funniest home movies?

II. An Oxymoron Called Free Speech

I'm sorry the ones who seem the most criminal
to me are those who turn their backs knowing
exactly what's happening you know the kind
who never once say sorry their whole life

III. Tweet Tweet Tweet

We need to just finally physically remove
the commander-in-chief i mean not like soon
or some time in the near future but immediately
like with a freaking wrecking ball be perfect poetic
justice for this real estate hospitality mogul
don't care how we do it the national guard
the state militia some giant bug zapper
tranquilizer gun one of those arch-villain
cattle prods or contraptions that shoots
out some knock-out potion put him in a
gigantic milkshake like they did to batman
and the boy wonder or maybe some hot-air
balloon that fucked-up corrupt wizard man
behind the curtain went into used helicopter

they put millhouse nixon in and just fucken
fly him the hell out of here and whisk him back to
his criminal empire reality show penthouse in the stars

IV. Candy Dates

Who would ever think the time would come
when billionaires would show up on my e-mail
and tell me they were the right man for the job?

V. Bazooka

What next?
bazooka joe
replaced with
the caption–
"no quid
pro quo!"

VI. What Got Bill Shakespeare

Politics is honesty turned inside-out
human nature and personality at its worst
remember that game you used to play as a kid
called opposites, he-said she-said, telephone
or for that matter not even returning calls?

#49

Where the hell are our real true-blue so-called
politicians who are supposed to represent the will
of the people not taking at all this climate change
global warming crisis seriously as ain't gonna
be like some blown-up version to the opening
of *gilligan's island* with gilligan and the skipper
being tossed back and forth by the currents on
some universal studio skiff fighting some vicious
storm on the high seas with a fighting chance more
like i swear some sort of *planet of the ape* noah's ark

ain't gonna get another chance at it
like discovering marie osmond's
bones in the desert of las vegas

#50

Where are our chris kringles to tell us to try gimbals
as felt back then, was all so much classier, keen and cool
when it was macy's & gimbals, woolworths & wannamakers

#51

You can talk of the bomb
you can talk of vietnam
you can talk of the presidents
(of the united states of america)
you can talk of assassinations
(in the united states of america)
you can talk of the war in iraq
you can talk of the war in afghanistan
you can talk of addictions like cocaine
and opiates eating and sexual fantasy
but what it always comes down to
in the end everything we live and die
(and i suppose fight) for is that one
moment is that image is the folklore
and one fleeting glance of a woman's
raw naked body no denying from top
to bottom however you look however
you like it her silhouetted portrait
planted in the alley in the valley
on the seashore in the mountains
what dreams and fantasy are made of
everything else is pure bullshit and denial

a radio suddenly switched on in coney island
with the sound of the waves in the background

sputtering planes suddenly showing up out of
nowhere bearing banners for suntan lotion & beer

#52

The happiest i ever remember myself being
hustling a yellow taxi graveyard shift in nyc
picking up this huge scandanavian family being
real nice and kind and down to earth and seemed
up for practically anything and remember driving
like some perfectly skilled kill or be killed madman
stuffed in there like sardines in a can while i swear
making every single light swerving nonstop back
and forth instinctively in and out of the cars taking
no prisoners not giving a damn without a mean bone
in my body (them actually appreciating it that much
more as if it was some sort of spontaneous liberating
experience in the land of america) while they were all
laughing out of control collectively hysterically as one
like this craziness was all a part of the experience they
were supposed to have of the image of all those ole
classic shoot 'em up black & white gangster films in
the back of a cab and glad to provide it and be a part
of it and when i screeched to a halt to end the tour
they all couldn't stop bawling and were just simply
thankful and grateful (while this in my opinion was
really getting to know the culture and people) and
think may have even made the declaration all of a
sudden from that scene from the movie *the in-laws*–
"the eagle has landed!" which they also appreciated
think the best time i probably had in i can't tell you…

#53

For the most part kids do follow "the golden rule"
(not so much so or true for their elders) as well as
those infamous regulations and exact directions
to a t, think about all those games we played as
a kid during recess (without adult supervision)
ringo-leevio having to capture a peer and if you
did would drag him in diligently to jail and accept
his fate, red rover with the opposing team calling
you over and running roughshod determined trying
to break through their line of defense of hands all
clasped together, the love and passion of kickball
which meant the world, and pick-up football and
basketball and if didn't follow that code or the sort
who was caught constantly complaining developed
something of a rotten reputation but interestingly
not really so much so in adulthood where it ironically
seems to be all about one-upping and competition
and cutting corners 'at all costs' as corruption
almost encouraged, while think it would be so
much more apropos if the rules and regulations
were posted on each and every office door…

#54

An abbreviated hx of amerika

scenes from the gun range
scenes from the golf range

one made to make you feel secure
one made to make you feel safe

having great difficulty making the distinction
between these two so-called forms of sanity

as look there goes the spotless citizens
coming out their church and country club

what happened to our humphrey
bogarts and edward g. robinsons

tarzan & abbott & costello
atticus finch like some

father figure fine upstanding
citizen there to save the day?

#55

Postcards of mermaids & seashores & the life & times
of those surviving studs who stood on top of each other's
shoulders in those human pyramids, waterskiing in a life
of leisure & the hx of the world, perfectly-sculpted with
slicked-back hair, grins & a whole life ahead of them

Love's not caring to be remembered
but sure as heck not forgotten…

#56

Post World War II Amerika:
(exchanging trauma for drama)

how many clean-cut boys can be stuffed
in a telephone booth trying to break records?

how many hours can you dance in a row
at the sock hop in the gymnasium without
passing-out making a spectacle of yourself?

how many goldfish can be swallowed in one sitting?

how many homes can be pre-fabricated
and staked-up in a couple hours in the suburbs
cookie-cutter style on dead ends in shangri-la?

how many drive-ins with great big screens in the middle of the
deep dark evening of romance & monsters & aliens invading?

how many girls on roller skates rolling straight
to their destination over to the open windows of
make-out cars with cheeseburgers & cherry coke?

how many solid citizens become morphine & sex addicts
due to all the business-like sales advertising & publishing
pressure having to make their quotas and just that one good
experience blasts them off to the stars to whole other realities
& galaxies making them want to keep on going & never give up?

how many fordham baldies badgering bullies rumored to shave
heads if they catch you and carve their initials into your skull
making you not want to show up for school and prefer to
just be part of the peanut gallery of crazy hollering kids
all joining in for that hymn–"it's howdy-doody time!"

how many manage to save up enough after selling sofas
all week at *macy's* to treat their family on sunday to chinese
and just order the same ole thing which is a #7 and can always
expect the exact same form of instant-gratification which is a

steaming eggroll, pork fried rice, and piping sweet
& sour chicken going to sleep under the influence?

#57

To me one of the most meaningful episodes of *happy days*
was when richie cunningham was just standing there at
the foul line all alone in his short shorts and had to just
sink one to send it into overtime and the ball went all
around the rim and out and was instantly transformed
from a hero to a goat and the stands all cleared out
even his best friends potsie and ralph until he was
just left there standing all alone in a dark gymnasium
staring off in a state of shock with no one at all to help
him out and to me just feels like the grand metaphor for
existence even when you got a heart of gold and the best
of intentions none of your friends or family around even
treat you like a total stranger when needing them the most

#58

So i guess in the long-run you just sort of
see yourself as one of those self-portraits
with your arms crossed divorced from one
of those infamous class photos of pals and
acquaintances with missing teeth and cute
and corny holy sacred smiles and a whole
wild life ahead of them from your bunk in
summer camp somewhere in the action
adventure madness between youth and
adolescence from that ole time baseball
team with those very serious and earnest
expressions and handlebar moustaches
from your military battalion and wonder
if they give some sort of medal of honor
for all the fucked-up abusive shit of what
life does to you and forced to go it alone
and now stand alone as some sole survivor
social observer independent thinker philosopher

#59

I have discovered freud's 'wit and its relation to the unconscious'
is directly related to an individual's arrested stage of development
could write a whole list of neuroses, phobias, rituals & superstitions

#60

In fact almost all conflicts and forms
of abnormal psychology, that being
psychodynamics, family dysfunction,
psychodrama, maladaptive thinking
(if not chemical) stems from those
who have never left their social or
cultural, psychosocial environment
(or been exposed to other elements
and modes of thinking and conflict
resolution, thus in fact, in truth and reality
have 'closed minds') while absurdly become
actors in a play that they're not even aware of

#61

How to cure self-doubt, paranoia & melancholia

1. walk down hall to light woodburning stove

2. throw in the funnies & obituaries

3. consider past girlfriends

4. johnny cash & bob dylan

5. call up *kfc* to see if they're serving thanksgiving

6. go to *expedia* like you used to for ibm and stats
   for the n.y. metropolitans to book a room down
   in the magical kingdom, somewhere between
   the near and remote future; maybe even rent
   a car so can explore the boulevard of orlando
   and stock up at one of those great big immaculate
   southern supermarkets let's say like *piggly wiggly*

7. buy a brand new pair of *pumas* for no apparent reason

#62

In the suburbs the people seem subhuman
way below the baseline (of humanity) of
communicating and processing and they
spread gossip and rumors too; the roots
of illusion and core nucleus of satire

#63

That red rose light of emergency constantly
blinking on the bat phone, while alfred
the butler having dozed-off a long time
ago due to a morphine and chemical
dependency problem right around
the bewitching hour off bottles of
after dinner brandy down in the
bat cave feeling no pain in the
renovated man cave of the
bruce wayne manor…

#64

I still though want to not get to know
those poor souls wasting away dying
off in their split-levels with shutters
fallen in the hills of silence and solitude
after those storms of the seasons leave
them glistening in dew until blue eternity

the homes like bizarre postmodern bones
found at some haunted post-apocalyptic
excavation of a strange savage suburbia

#65

Real problem often quagmire with suburbia
is everyone's fighting to try and be or look
as safe and secure as possible (they'll put in
alarms and sprinkler systems) as this is their
real-life dream and fantasy and long-term goal
but none of this so-called terror-try ("plots" of
land) or so-called solitude is natural and of course
with human nature and the petty aggressive competitive
one-upping nature of neighbors seeming to thrive off
gossip and rumors (and everyone literally in everyone
else's business acting like perfectionists to cover up
all the imperfections of the deep-down emptiness
insecurities and real-life "vacancy" of the things
that plague them) which all eventually comes back
to haunt them (in the deepest depths of the evening
and early morning routines) triggering and touching
on all those existential feelings of severe and profound
loneliness and alienation or a silence which is so artificial
(ridiculous and fictional) feels desperate almost suicidal

Contrary, ironically, i once knew a black girl whose name
was sunshine (met in my taxi while driving the graveyard)
and lived at *the times square hotel* in the back alley but
somehow managed to make herself happy (with a history
of abuse) and was a buddhist and would do her daily chants
in front of her shrine every morning and every night, while
people were literally getting knocked-off and dropping like flies
yet somehow made all that damage and tragedy seem worthwhile

mulch gets spread all around the virgin mary
to make it look all immaculate and more alive

#66

ibid: The local cable reads something
like–"regular meeting" and looks like
all the barely breathing brooding silent
polite old timer uptight upstanding
citizen plato cave dwellers gathered
around the great big mahogany table
(with great big murals on the wall of
similar historical foreboding figures)
all a cross of wanting to put a bullet
in their brain go insane or way too sane
worrying about their broken marriages
or broken realities all until some young
pure dove goddess angel all of a sudden
shows up on the tv screen like some sweet
sci-fi queen for some sort of symposium
as if giving some kind of bas-mitzvah
or sweet sixteen speech and seems
like the blush of reality all of a sudden
creeps back to their cheeks giving them
some reason to go on living even crack
a few jokes and reach an instant simple
resolution been bickering over for ages
pick up their notes and get up in silence
and vanish into thin air as if at last in a flash
no longer there at the end of broadcasting day

ibid: These days the interviewers are so bad
(putting people on the instant defensive)
seems more like an interrogation but if
the individual can't even finish their
thought or sentence what really is
the whole point and purpose? is it
to try and rattle (and intimidate
and manipulate) someone so
much so as just to conform to
their exact beliefs and thoughts
thus you honestly really don't
get to know a thing about them
just passive-aggressive and
fragmented and get a whole
hell of a lot of arguing but
absolutely no argumentation.
in fact there's absolutely no tact
at all while even back in the day
when you had such people like
that conservative william f. buckley
he spoke in such a stimulating self-
soothing tone (gave the impression
as though he was curious and interested
even though often coming off awfully
snide and sarcastic) you'd at least be
able to get their point of view and then
can present and lay-out exactly where
they're coming from and thus have
a platform for intellectual rapport

I think it was andy warhol put it best when he said
with that very monotone cleverness–"why don't
you just give me the question *and* the answer…"

ibid:

Chaplin, kerouac tried to keep
their high as long as they could.
they tell you if you fall off the horse
to get right back on but not always
as simple as it sounds if knew all
the damage done; i've known artists
who lived in the park far more astute
& sharp (wise & street smart) than any
college professor with their doctorate

ibid:

At best the tourist is a cut-out figure
(non-action figure) with a whole list
of affectations which include aloofness
and arrogance, sexless, soulless,
very prim and proper, obvious, with
their contraptions trying to predictably
(absurdly) capture the moment (in time)
of 'the starving artist' who for one reason
or another forced to go it alone and ironically
sacrificed his life for the greater good of man

all the bullshit and bureaucracy and pain and suffering
the isolated soul has to go through and endure (a life
of stigmatization and scorn) just to create beauty

ibid:

I see life alot like one of those horrible world problems
from back in childhood asking such inane shit like if
dick takes off and races at a clip of 80 mph from his
home to his job and jane (being a similar snob and slob)
at the exact same speed at what point will they eventually
(crash and) meet while you deep down inside already turned
off knowing completely out for self and a bunch of greedy selfish
tourists who in fact don't give a damn about a thing around them
while always being something of a romantic turn towards bigger
and better things like fantasizing about your older sister's girlfriends

ibid:

Why with that expression 'coming around
full circle' they always seem to attach
a positive connotation, as to me just
means you've come back to the exact
same starting point with the exact
same amount of pain and suffering

ibid: a strange takeoff of that red wheel
barrow william carlos williams poem...

Remember as a teenager peddling my bicycle
through the hills and hedgerow and backstreets
of bath with all the wild chickens in the drizzle
and a walkman covering my ears listening to
springsteen emotionally singing pleading–
"she's singing! singing! singing! singing!"
and all i could think about was my future

got sent home a day early
to laguardia for stealing...

ibid: They used to say such shit to me like–
"i can't get a straight answer out of this kid"
if they only knew how i had gotten so used
to dealing with so many crooked influences

ibid:

Making a documentary about your life
and it's one of those silent films where they
show you turning around and pacing a couple
steps in each direction and suddenly drawing your
gun and shooting and then falling to your knees weeping
as apparently it was a clean miss and got all your friends
in the human pyramid but upon reflection due to the most
petty traits and characteristics of human nature left first
and deserted and abandoned and show you slowly getting
up a bit more defensive and guarded dancing slapstick while
you're about to be officially endorsed by not only the warden
with his windchimes in the window of the prison but all the boys
of mistaken identity serving a lifetime bid you went all out for
giving them their start in the business as in the recovery period
walking your dog through the cemetery right next door
to miniature golf and the drive-in where you are
superimposed and illuminated up on the big
screen having made something of yourself

ibid:

An ad comes up on my e-mail
for mature quality singles
sounds like a horrible
appetizer for the
adult world…

ibid:

Why whenever people like lovers or mothers
or idiot authority figures get really pissed-off
they exclaim such ridiculous shit like "mister!"
and keep on repeating that over and over like
they're hyperventilating or some very formal
manifesto with a dangling participle at the end
of each sentence and think if you're really that
mad at me why do you keep on referring to me
as mister and believe they are far more lost
and desperate than can ever be imagined

ibid:

Those speaking with such formality (to others) are usually
not deserving of it (a psychodynamic or defense-mechanism
called 'reactive-formation' where one talks in blatant opposites)
most likely passive-aggressively overcompensating while voicing
their anger and frustration (incapable for one reason or another
of making any sort of concrete or intimate connection) in fact
linguistically going through the motions, trying to keep
their very fragile and 'formal' demeanor and distance

like the leftovers or remainder of that cliché expression–
'you never get a second chance to make a first impression'

ibid:

Most customs and traditions come from superstition...
all those things pawned, fumbled, and not quite making
it, passed down from generation to generation; the spirit
of some damaged raconteur still going through the motions
(and rituals) trying to put all those shattered things back
together again. the young man sardonically claims when he
sees the procession and parade of old people–"they're walking!"

ibid:

I guess my dad
was right about
a couple things
how family are
the few people
who can truly
be trusted
& believed
(i think…)
we used to have
these mowing guys
from the old country
(of sicily)
ralph & lenny
i was actually
quite fond of
who were a
father & son team
& used to tell me how
ralph was always just
kvetching nonstop
about something
& that's how i guess
i just now view a lot of
life like ralph & lenny
always finding some
reason to complain
or if you're lucky
even getting
back to you

#67

Those envious of you
make their music
make their blues
by staying out
of touch with
you like all that static
between radio stations
on some bleak overcast
afternoon but who really
gives a flying as tune
in to vivaldi's violins

"i'm going to chicago
that's the last place
my baby stayed…"

#68

Advertising In America:

commercials of slapstick violence
sell insurance in amerika (made to
make you anxious and agitated then
instantly purchase the product like
some safe & secure savior) which
ironically seems very similar to
our domestic and foreign policy

"Where are you going?"
"Nowhere…"
"Do you mind if I come along?"

-American Graffiti

American Hx: Act I

On the dead end in the homeowner's association
one of the listed pluses and assets for curbside
appeal is the towering pines in the tall woods
but just like neighbors in amerika there's always
something to gripe about, just like that very practical
life insurance salesman who prefers and spouts wish
could just all be cut down and live far closer to town as
known to be something of a control freak and obsessive
compulsive cleaner and just doesn't like all those annoying
pesky pine needles, and always the first one to have his
christmas tree put on the curb right after the holiday ends
so now imagine a perfect shangrila dead end surrounded
by just tree stumps far closer to the stripmall composed
of your dunkin donuts, sears, and super stop & shop

Well what else can you ask for? let's make a deal…

American Hx: Act II

I never was very good at being a grownup...
they always just seemed so serious and formal
while never really took particular interest or cared
to play any of those roles, looking like they were
all posing for some pathetic photo (as though trying
to preserve their absurd mortality) like at a country
club or shriners convention or dinner party yet still
all seemed so resentful and hostile, like some never
ending long-winded riddle with a sadistic punchline
that does not quite deliver, like having some drinking
problem or on the brink of divorce; everyone looking
proverbially 'cheated on' drained by what life has done
to them; the women just standing with the women and
guys standing with the guys never quite having grown
up from the schoolyard all in disguise like a pack of toy
poodles sniffing out the trail for toy soldiers going in for
the kill; ghosts desperately clinging onto some form of
sex appeal now ironically substituted for 'small talk'
and all the trivial things they conquered (and proudly
took advantage of) in their kill or be kill field of dead
lines and quotas and sales while always just so much
more preferred and got so much more hanging-out
with the help or the babysitters; the buzzed fiddler
heading up to the roof looking out over all of bleak
suburbia which is composed of just two 'flesh-colored'
tulips barely having survived the seasons; skeletons
leaning up against the deep dark secrets and shadows
of the backyard fence, all that shit eventually in the
long-run that'll eat you up and kill you if you don't...

American Hx: Act III

Too often the kawkasian cult/ure in amerika
living in their absurd insular delusional worlds
mean-spirited and miserable thrive off trying to
embarrass or humiliate or alienate their neighbor
while if you call that biblical, does not this make
them the anti-christ? white devil? (scapegoating
trying to turn them all into 'freaks' and 'strangers'
instantly judging, gaslighting as if they're a danger)
the american indian used to righteously claim how
they go out of their way to try and confuse you, or
like the black scholars say, always seem to do their
shit from a very safe distance; it is not by coincidence
their critical and parasitic body language and expressions
(which too often seems to present as hostile full of hatred)
always appear to indicate that you're somehow infringing
on their territory (that lovely american phenomenon of
privilege and entitlement; the soulless tourist like you're
there just to serve them, and how dare you even consider
being anywhere in their area, or with their self-absorbed
egocentric clinical narcissism 'one of them' when couldn't
care less nor ever crossed your mind or consciousness, and
swear seen more than all them put together, and don't have
a clever bone in their body; sub/urban/knights with this
mock apple pie reality) sociologically, characterologically,
not too ironically, the exact same behavioral pattern for the whole
spoiled obnoxious nauseating family passed down from generation
to generation, rotten to the core from the roots up and when you
approach them (like a wind in a storm) seem instantly to fold
turn scared (even scared of themselves) on-the-run, die off
and not so brave or tough anymore or so laissez-faire in telling
their silly sissy secrets, while now the cowards and hypocrites
and opportunists they are instantly looking to make deals and
bargains and compromise, crying out for love and support

conveniently turn to family lawyer and family court
(with no sex appeal make their whole list of appeals)
and make their token annual charitable donations to
relieve their guilty conscious (to prove how 'virtuous')
hopefully even get some sort of tax break or deduction but
what happens when the whole lot are already soulless lost causes?

American Hx: Act IV

A Case Study Of "The Success"

People who to get places having spent a whole lifetime
of lying suddenly when the truth hits them (in some
form or another) honestly go into instant denial
and then come up with a whole other pack of lies
and rationalizing which is their illusory truth and
reality (they are known to literally change their
story multiple times within seconds and get
instantly defensive and then go on the offensive).
anyone who happens to remind them of such events
becomes 'a menace' and suspicious due to their threat-
ening nature and the possible unmasking of their secret

American Hx: Act V

A Case Study Of The All-Knowing Anacronym

We live in a time where everyone seems obliged to have to tell us about their sexuality and party (which to me sounds a bit self-absorbed or form of self-aggrandizement) and think just preferred the seventies when things were a little more mysterious and left room for the imagination

American Hx: Act VI

A Case Study Of "The Outcast"

I always got along best with kids whose parents
were never around and had no way of getting
home from the train station, introspective,
sensitive and self-sufficient whose emptiness
and bleak existence almost felt like they had
so much more to say and offer, maybe wearing
some bandana around their head, handsome and
sacred and having to find some creative way never
complaining to get to that long-lost lonely destination
which always seemed somewhere nowhere out there
on the fictional shadowy outskirts of the seasons

American Hx: Act VII

A Case Study On Suburbia

A note stuck to the outside of door reads
"for the love of god, mow your lawn"

American Hx: Act VIII

A Case Study On Suburbanization

They are putting up another one of those
massive immaculate pristine self-soothing
southern malls meant to be the cultural hub
(which i suppose is all well and good positive
and productive for the economy but still seems
a bit soulless and monochromatic, like some
gigantic mannequin thriving and feeding off
instant-gratification) is this what they refer
to in that similar absurd and awful period of
reconstruction, very convenient and commercial
but seem just as guilty as any of those carpet-
baggers they claim came down just to rob and
make a quick buck and take advantage, while
honestly doesn't feel like any south i remember
with row upon row of imitative prefabricated
plantation homes in such plush and manicured
subdivisions of suburbia getting swallowed
up by the biotech and banking industry

American Hx: Act IX

A Case Study Of Spirit(s)

How would t.s. eliot dylan thomas have felt
when they suddenly smelt the sweet scent
from seeping stamen bleeding blossoming
magnolia rippling spilling outside the motel
door down in the bible belt something don't
think they had too much of out on the english
countryside or wales would have loved to have
seen the innocent child-like look on their faces
at 6:02 in the misty morning right on the border of
bleak & beautiful north & south carolina something
i knew o too well for lo all those lost lonesome years
down in the big easy penetrating and permeating my
spiritual being most of all the wild haunted slapping
shutters of my torn tormented soul and stayed with
me whether i was aware of it or not somewhere
between those animated ancient gargoyles
perched atop the mausoleums on bourbon
and the madwomen like phantoms sleep
walking on canal doing their daily rounds
taking deserted strolls downtown mumbling
manic mantras towards twain's mississippi
where i'd spend hours brooding and felt all
those spirits run through me never knowing
would stay with me till the bittersweet end

American Hx: Act X

A Case Study On Angst

You get married and end up doing
some pretty ridiculous, crazy shit
like start taking one-a-day vitamins
purchasing all these different types
of insurances; head out the house
in the pitch-black, maybe a couple
stars still leftover in the sky hearing
your neighbor's automatic sprinkler
go on (knowing he's practically
ironically just as robotic) and
couldn't feel anymore alone
forced to go to barbecues
standing around with other
neighbors who are complete
strangers and you just have
absolutely nothing to say to
them and just prefer taking strolls
with your kid and babysitter; end
up working a 10 hour day at a place
you can't stand including all the bum
paduhbumpa traffic during rush hour...
the classic oxymoron and onomatopoeia
and head home once again in the darkness,
drained, exhausted, a former ghost of yourself
past the lit-up dog track and mall (gas stations
glowing looking like the pot of gold at the end
of the rainbow, the only place where you can
truly be independent and left alone) feeling
your whole life pass right in front of you,
press the control for the electric garage,
crawl up the basement stairs to your angel
wife and child and when she asks you how
your day was can't get a word out your mouth;
you know when you sit down you're never gonna
get up again and all you care about is getting the
scores, as if that might make much of a difference
in your world and see all the news on the ticker below

roll by and the death toll of some soldier killing 21
in a rampage, while robert conrad the "wild wild west"
star at 93 dies as your mind, heart and soul doesn't budge.

There was this bukowski poem— don't remember
which one it was where he was giving some poetry
reading at a college, and right after it was over in
the dark literally got lost while staggering drunken
across the quad, and felt like i was really able
to relate and that's just a lot of what life is
barely hanging on just trying to get back
and find your way home to the mirage

American Hx: Act XI

A Case Study Of Higher Learning

So the sorority tells you to be a slut
to not have an independent thought
can only fuck certain boys
from certain fraternities
call this higher learning
and eventually end up only
marrying a doctor or lawyer
moving straight to the suburbs
bearing 2-3 children and cloning
soulless seductive saintly daughters

halftime report: the apocalypse sponsored
by *xfinity* awards for everything with trophies
handed back & forth by fake blondes in sequins
all with the exact same sculpted health club bodies

cowboys now have degrees from good colleges

taylor swift like some manufactured goddess
doing her swift mysterious madonna/whore
cha-cha-cha move (just like janet and every
other choreographed cartoon character) where
suddenly snaps her head staring straight at you

American Hx: Act XII

In all those *hgtv* shows where people
buy up properties and homes and in
the end when decide which one they chose
i swear all i ever really care about are the dogs
(as know the humans are just going to find
a way to be all-knowing, obnoxious, take it
all for granted and be ungrateful; it just comes
natural) those cooking shows where they put on
that "i can't believe how good this tastes" look,
sometimes even prematurely before they bite into
their creation and wonder why they never show one
of those ole time barbecues where the brothers are
playing their sunday radio; al green, the godfather
of soul, "poppa was a rolling stone," while in this
country we love to throw around such political
and intellectual terms and expressions like 'a
working and functioning democracy' and promise
you i have experienced both and can't begin to tell
you which one i have felt more a part of, included,
and belonged, as ain't that just really what class
culture and civilization 101 is supposed to be all about?

American Hx: Act XIII

unit a,

Out here in the mountains people get a hankering
for the sea and becomes tradition where like once
a year head out to the cape to get their fill of seafood
lobster and new england clam chowder yet for me
kind of like bartelby the scrivener 'i prefer not to'
as spent way too much time out there with that whole
lot of soulless tourists stuck in bumpadabumpa traffic
in east sandwich so instead just turn on *hgtv* to like
lakefront bargains or purchasing waterfront property
on the gulf with these idiot happily-ever-after couples
even if just to be on the ocean it means only a slight glimpse
of the beach from their tiny terrace in one of those monstrous
monochromatic felliniesque concrete slab condominiums
on the ocean with prefurnished units which all look exactly
the same with pink and blue pastel paintings of the seashore
on the wall and always seem to choose those and perfectly
content being one of these cookie-cutter conformist clones
with all the perfect proper postcard amenities and blue tropical
drinks to placate them and keep their sanity having ridiculously
convinced themselves of happiness when they take their
mandated romantic strolls along the ocean at sunset

unit b,

Log cabin living
seeing where they
purchase it for like
$1,375,000 (this log
cabin in kwaint amerika)
their token wine tasting
in their token vineyard
and think how much
they just don't deserve it
and so much more the natives
(who most likely will treat them
like slaves leaving them to question

their time on earth and being) who
grew up there in the radiant holy
mountains & rivers of appalachia
serving them their fresh blueberry
muffins & blend of gourmet coffee

American Hx: Act XIV

It seems to me from what i see in the land of the free
the best way for different cultures and minorities to
fit in and acclimate and acculturate is to lower their
baseline of traits and characteristics with obnoxious
expressions and body language (imitative affectations)
to prove they can be just as indifferent and alienate like
the white girl ("valley girl") then alien hating just like them

American Hx: Act XV

Why do struggling actors take on certain such roles
like becoming bartenders (i've seen whole barrooms
full of struggling actors) while thus going back to the ole
geometric equation of the law of opposites would that then
preclude struggling bartenders just being really poor actors?

American Hx: Act XVI

One wonders if back in the day when they
used to sit back in their vinyl *chevrolets*
at the drive-in movie if they ever fell in
love more with the stars up on the big screen
as opposed to the girls sitting by their sides
they were obligated to make the moves on
and when driving home thinking more so
of some great brilliant dramatic soliloquy
able to relate to given by like brando
in "on the waterfront" james stewart in
"it's a wonderful life" even troy donahue
in "a summer's place" waking up in the
morning still in their long johns not so
much convinced of descarte's proof
of existence of 'i think therefore i am'
calling her up out of some sort of displaced
passion telling her how much she meant to him

American Hx: Act XVII

For me natural red heads
are the real blonde bomb
shells when brunettes
started obsessively
dying their hair
in the 50's for
purposes of
seduction
& sex appeal
as for me i'll take
any day a natural
fiery red head &
all the beauty
that goes on
down there

that there is true
amerikan kulture

American Hx: Act XVIII

Looking way back to those days
when i used to date and might
have had friends of the opposite
persuasion who always wanted
to set me up with fellow employees
or acquaintances for those infamous
blind dates the dynamic always
seemed so see-through and
sleazy like these desperate
ladies who had just come off
really bad marriages or some
were even like these real
successful business women
in publishing or advertising
some i swear were therapists
and had not had it in ages even
once had a girl who confessed to
me how her and her friends used
to say if they hadn't gotten laid
in like a year or so were like virgins
all over again and in this strange
sleazy perverse way i somehow
felt the actual victim to that age
old adage the sacrifice of a virgin

American Hx: Act XIX

It was sad but during that soulless error
of the eighties there were girls called
coke whores often some of the most
down-to-earth innocent looking ones
(which i suppose was part of that
whole je ne sais quois) like
the ivory girl going for hers

American Hx: Act XX

As a guy now remember walking around
with my mom in the lady's locker room
at the y in the early 70's those young
moms in their early 30's just walking
around so freely and naturally gabbing
it up and giggling (always seeming so nice
and kind and welcoming) with their fine jewish
liberal bosoms of all different shapes & sizes
whole swaths of cat's cradle macrame moist
dewy petal pussies and now the exact women
we get set up with for blind dates (accountants,
psychiatrists) and hunger after taking their dogs
on long lonely early evening strolls beneath the
stars through cemeteries looking for just one guy
who they can rely on and won't let them down
(and even settle down) and drive them crazy

American Hx: Act XXI

Aww what to say really not much to say
about those absurd and pathetic parents
who just seem so lost and miserable and
bickering or even worse yet going through
the motions, pushing their kids in the play-
ground completely detached and disinterested
in everything around them (some even create
their own exclusive culture and hierarchy
of which i guess supposed to feel honored
i always try to avoid like the plague) yikes!
really can't think of anything or any place
i'd rather not be while always prefer so
much more that kind ole man walking
his blind seeing-eye dog through town
both sort of hobbling around and just
trying to get by who appear so much
more benign and content without the burden
of any of these ridiculous influences of existence

American Hx: Act XXII

Nixon claimed to be the best bowler
in the white house; he also purported
to hate jews while he was surrounded
by them as always found it funny all
those who took the fall for him and
ended up doing bids and him seeing
absolutely no time in prison ending
up flying back to his condo in nyc
just like what we got today how
history has a tendency to absurdly
repeat itself like social and political
satire shakespeare's tragic comedies

American Hx: Act XXIII

Our next president should be some
stunning gorgeous tomboy with short
hair a killer smile in form-fitting jeans
and hightop *chuck taylor's* who works
at the local hardware store and keeps
the old timers coming back entranced
enamored even perhaps flattered and
delusional that she might really like
even love them and have a possible
chance as she'll just sit back on
airforce one with that killer
coquettish smile to one of
those infamous world summits
or another, neither a democrat
nor republican but real representative
of what it means whatever the heck
it means to be a true-blue american

American Hx: Act XXIV

I don't know— this presidential election
where they all just stand on the debate
stage behind their podium trying to give
off an heir of confidence they all look a
little like clark kent with a pained grin
stuck in the phone booth trying to
change into superman while this
madman megalomaniac lex luther
and his fellow sycophant arch-villains
seem to have brainwashed and cast
a spell taken full control over the corrupt
metropolis mafia syndicate with their threats
and hits of might-over-right kryptonite and
want to believe like some greater and higher
form of justice and good and morals and ethics
can save us but each day start losing just a little
more faith and hope as the suspense keeps building
up and wondering if clark kent can just manage to get
out of that phone booth. they claim democracy at times
can be something of a sloppy process as you're just waiting
for that one simple courageous man with his push broom
perhaps like some old retired boxer to sweep up the alley

American Hx: Act XXV

I think the next primary since the whole thing
is just really one big damn circus should be
held in like atlantic city or coney island and
have like a hotdog eating contest and see who can
set the record for stuffing the most frankfurters down
their pie hole who can swallow swords and spit fire
who can stand the longest up on top of stilts in their
red white and blue costume and top hat who's willing
to be a real man of the people and get shot with a water
gun sticking their head through the mouth of a clown
or shot down and dunked in some grand tank of water
and when they're done get to present their best argument
and background and political promises in the center of
the ring being circled by elephants and dwarfs and freaks
the one problem though they'd most likely be no challenge
for the grand barker of them all already decked-out in orange
face clown makeup with his bullhorn and ten-gallon and toy
gun having no conscience or conflict at all with spouting lies
one by one by one by one as just what comes natural and
been stretching the truth and abusing power since day one

American Hx: Act XXVI

They seem to be talking alot on the news
these days with the upcoming elections
about certain swaths of the country lay
of the land demographics and populations
as apparently it always seems to come
down to having to appeal to the suburban
white woman (as you think they're still
manipulating and what did they do to
deserve this?) and think if i was ever
running for a seat i'd have to really be
running and running and running and
running considering all the damage
inflicted by some of those really
crazy insane dramatic white women
i knew from back in the day; wonder
if they have a specific category for
any these types of ladies as for me
always were the ones who pushed
me over the edge and in my opinion
might really be able to sway the election

American Hx: Act XXVII

I think i've always preferred those long lines
waiting outside the diabetic bakery and *otb*
in carrol gardens, brooklyn than those lines
waiting to vote for political candidates, as
the former just seems so much more real
and sincere and down-to-earth and weird
and the latter so much more opportunistic
and fake looking to be saved, while eventually
in the long-run when find their life just has not
changed and exactly the same always love to
blame and act betrayed so i don't know for me
the first always ironically just felt more like a
part of the culture and community contributing
to society and a real-life democracy returning
home with their tattered, punch-drunk tickets
like the leftover confetti to some funeral
procession, or the wilted flowers of some
pathetic lost stud still desperately searching
for love, brooding, humble, not all-knowing and
higher-than-holy, but just kind of slowly dying
going through the motions, accepting their fate
and you always knowing exactly who they are
and all of their stories (how frank just not the
same after he got struck by that truck, eternally
out of it, down on his luck or those old time
merchant marines from the neighborhood
with drinking problems but with hearts of
gold yet somehow strangely enough felt
you could trust) while the others just
seemed more out-of-touch, out for self
and their bank accounts, and acted all hoity-
toity; the most obvious and boring kind of glory
while when it comes down to the nitty-gritty
take any day those wasting away on the corner

American Hx: Act XXVIII

This morning somehow white devils
got through and got messages from
eric trump and karl rove and newt
gingrich infestating my computer.
they're like a bunch of pests and
cockroaches and wonder if my
exterminator can handle this?

addendum #1:

No disrespect but every fucken president
i ever knew and grew up with from nixon
to this fucken idiot, resembled something
like burt & ernie from "sesame street" that's
all i'm saying signed sealed delivered eeek!

addendum #2:

Our emperor came to be
cause he couldn't take
a joke dished out at a
roast and introduced
himself to the public
as a man of the people
coming down his
golden escalator

isn't that how most
rich privileged kid
dictators got
their start?

American Hx: Act XXIX

I don't know— maybe i'm wrong
but back in the day it just seemed
so much more natural and classier
fluid and historical how we chose
and voted for our president as now
it just seems so cheap and shit
with all these commercials
and advertisements meant
to try and brainwash the public
and masses like just ripping out
a couple coupons from the paper
of what's been subliminally embedded
in our subconscious; the defeated and
deflated giving their concession speeches
as we return home with some surreal bag full
of everything-must-go basic staples and leftovers

American Hx: Act XXX

1. americans seem happiest when about to get appliances

2. very similar to the phenomenon of chinese

3. when reaching their token quota of 2-3 kids

4. (all of them forms of being reborn)

5. and move to dead ends and live happily ever after in the ribbons of barbecue smoke

6. on the proverbial fence using those couple extra bucks to put in a pool or renovating a basement

7. or going on one of those all-inclusive vacations to the caribbean for workaholic reasons socializing and integrating with the natives (to prove their diversity) who serve them drinks on the beach or authentic cuisine at the evening buffet (apparently made up of fire swallowers and tin drums) and humdrum suburban women pretending to be dancing all o la la taboo and risque with other suburban women trying to give the safe and secure impression (of folklore and false seduction) of being suddenly turned on

8. all with *hallmark* memories conveniently memorialized in photo albums

9. the commercials now show caucasians on dead ends backing out of their driveways with token electronic radar systems so they don't hit anyone and some idiot kid with his head down passing in the back just looking down deaf blind and dumb at his smartphone not seeing a single thing around him. class, what is wrong with this picture and culture and civilization? what has happened to instincts and the senses? does this seem like an upgrade and improvement or more so just some pseudo-glamorization of the archetype of 'truth' and 'virtue' of the caucasian in amerika?

10. sports and weather used to have something of a calming influence
    now they just make you all anxious and agitated with commercials
    of young up & coming entrepreneurs you cannot even relate
    to or connect with always seeming to be toasting each other

11. preferred *the little rascals* when baking a cake in the oven
    rising falling developing a life of its own with a boot in it

12. almost all illusions (like delusions of grandeur)
    stem from very lost empty places

13. like the suburbs/like suburbanization

14. like that sleazy statistic that man fantasizes
    about a woman almost every 12 seconds

15. like we're happiest when find out a past
    girlfriend finds out you found someone better

16. and just rings the phone and then hangs up
    and you know it's her and finally get closure

American Hx: Act XXXI

The police benevolent association calls up
asking for a donation and you simply snicker
and hang up the phone already having gotten
their quota trying to turn over a new leaf bringing
roses home from *the home depot* and when you
ask them why they stopped you tell you they don't
have to and they run the show returning home from
vacation having to pick up speed leaving the toll
booths tailing you all the way home working with
troubled kids all day long at the group home doing
the same just driving all through town the farms
and ocean so your toddler can get some shut eye
hiding behind the weeds beneath bridges dairy
creams colleges graveyards out there all by
your lonesome trying to land a second job

American Hx: Act XXXII

Weather Forecast:

fog, frogs...
nicknames change
for those you love
as time goes on
you took her to
go whitewater
rafting, gloucester
little later on dingle
peninsula, paris
and andalucia
still reminds
me never
got to see the
glassblowers
& flamenco
dancers…

American Hx: Act XXXIII

Man always talkin' bout moving mountains
i never wanted to move any mountain as was
more so satisfied & contented with that mountain
right there just staring straight down at me staring
up at that great big gorgeous majestic mountain
& rather cared that i was there forever & ever
& never be moved from that horizon; the big
top flying away all of a sudden into the great blue
sky leaving just the elephants & freaks stunned
& bewildered gun-shy to slowly stagger away
to the sea, while their ancestors staked-out
beneath the boardwalk as wilbur & orville
got all their best material simply watching
the wild birds dip & dive contemplating
over the cliffs of kill devil hills right around
that broken down motel where lost lovers
ostracized by their culture had secret rendez-
vous on the stilts of the ocean; darwin hunched
over taking his poloroid snapshots of crustacean
& sea turtles all eventually to metamorphosize
& transform to hawthorne wingo a 6'10 bench
warmer for the ny knickerbockers during
the 70's while the brothers smoked their
blunts in the blues just trying to get by

shakespeare holding up a skull of mayor laguardia…

American Hx: Act XXXIV

The boo-joie always
leave you hanging
babe ruth spent
the rest of his
remaining days
waiting for a call
from the front
office of the
ny yankees
that would
never come
from "the house
that ruth built"
and never even
got a return call

American Hx: Act XXXV

Alot of people don't know or realize
that when those guys buzz aldrin
and john glenn landed on the moon
were gonna try out some ole time
classic vaudeville punchline like
"you got a preacher and rabbi..."
but decided the last second with
the nature of political and social
unrest down on the planet earth to
just go with that 'one giant step for
mankind' then casually floated back
with a long eternal sigh while the first
thing they did when they got home to
their split-levels in the suburbs was to
just shower off the spacedust like some
convict just returning home from prison
and creep into the fetal position and take
a long catnap all the way to the following day
like some drained cabdriver after his graveyard
or mason jar of stewed fruit marinating in the icebox

static still on the idiot box
of some ballgame chicago
versus the new york mets

American Hx: Act XXXVI

Charlton heston still in a heap of rags
by the shore with the statue of liberty
and her torch poking out of the sand
and jon voight accepting an academy
award for best actor in *midnight cowboy*

American Hx: Act XXXVII

The kung-fu chinese movie theater
and literal warm sweltering summer
pork fried alley of hester st. lower east side

boys playing handball in draining sunlight…

American Hx: Act XXXVIII

It's crazy but i feel like
i finally made it after
i graduated yeshiva
and my fiancee
and i moved out
to rhode island
and i liked just
getting gas at
that shell station
cause i liked the
color of the sign
and was just on
that simple clean
corner overlooking
the navy shipyards
and was purely anonymous
and felt totally independent
getting a new start and no
longer underestimated
working on school street
at that mental health clinic
transporting myself back &
forth all day over the bridges
from the girl's group home
in newport to narangansett
to providence returning home
zombie-like wired and wasted
with secondary trauma a strange
sort of way to feel alive again
in our little cape at sundown

American Hx: Act XXXIX

On the weather channel i saw where a gigantic fish
was literally trying to swim across the road during
this major flood and this piece of white trash with
big bushy beard and sarcastic smile just picked him
up like he was starring in america's funniest home
videos as this big fish was just flapping around like
mad shocked and startled holding on for dear life
while his white trash friend with a gun in holster
part of his dress code just very conveniently started
taking a picture of them with his smart phone (lord
how times have changed since days of hemingway)
as was just hoping he might have the heart or soul
to consider tossing him back in and returning him
back to the river where he came from but never
seemed to cross his mind and the clip just ended
right there returning back to the weathercasters
who didn't seem to really care or make much
mention about anything having to do with
climate change or flooding or just that big
fish getting picked up against his own will
and volition on the road when all he was
trying to do bewildered and confused was get
on and mind his own and find his way back home

American Hx: Act XXXX

scenes from deep within the origami bomb...
scenes from the thimble there to collect rainwater
scenes from the diorama and screams in the shoebox
scenes from the dollhouse the remains of what is not
scenes from the tiny giants taking on a life in the terrarium
scenes from the line of toy soldiers there to serve and protect
and to preserve and never forget the spirit of the imagination

American Hx: Act XXXXI

I never really understood
that expression marriage
material as what exactly
would that look like the
funnies and obituaries?

American Hx: Act XXXXII

Marriage is her standing at the head
of the last supper table reading directly
from the board game directions (could
be *monopoly, battleship, sorry*) and him
with a gun to his head having died a long
time ago just trying to explain only cracks
jokes to try and make a connection and get
closer to her no different than when they first
met which is all he ever really meant and them
going back and forth in a ridiculous kafkaesque
argument deconstructing and having to prove
his purpose and intentions and breaking down
the semantics of the punchline while just prays
there might be those little dishes of jello in the
refrigerator to make everything alright again

American Hx: Act XXXXIII

She runs into a friend of hers
in the aisle of *walgreens* both
with stubbed toes and bandages
around their ankles ironically both
coming from broken households and
domineering overbearing emotionally
abusive mothers giving them klutzy
symptoms and eternally accident-prone
how does that slogan go again about being
'on the corner of happy and healthy?'

American Hx: Act XXXXIV

No one ever
said it'd be easy
always hated
when people
said such things
& spoke anecdotally
always left me hanging
famous last words of
holden p. caulfied
the speed limit
of crows
across the
field of snow
is there a
med to help
to forget
them all
everything
they stole
with no
return
address
sans
an op
iate ad
diction
some
where
between
o-hi-o
& af
ghan
istan
taking
a fleeting
train out
of town
during
the winter

past the
madmen
& schitz
ofrantics
smoking
cigarettes
on the platform
sir marcel proust
holed up in his
roost in paris
one of the first
in his day & age
to get one of those
contraptions where'd
hear live symphonies
cause could afford it
of vivaldi & wagner
scents & aroma
of menthol
to trigger
remembrances
& fight off neuroses

American Hx: Act XXXXV

Imagine jesus silhouetted
still hanging on the cross
no one having taken him
off due to might-over-right
(change of allegiance)
mentality of man…
nothing but that accordion
still trying to pay off and
monkey organ grinder
just trying to make it
the professional mourners
on strike again by the pyramids
the taking of pelham 1, 2, 3
10,000 motels on the sea
david bowie singing
"wild is the wind"

American Hx: Act XXXXVI

What a weird and wonderful dream being back in some dream
on a fine sunny day after school in the seventies and myself
seemingly set back somewhere in the bushes while seeing
this bright-eyed stunning girl in a sundress bounding back
and forth to the open window of lou reed just hanging out
in his car and myself instantly being attracted and falling
in love with her but having her declare i liked him even
though i kind of loved her because at that age and stage
didn't want to be burdened and bothered and held down
with the hang-ups and drama and karma of women or
more so just the seriousness and told her all about this
and said yeah she could tell him and make this work
and happen and thought it would really work out be-
tween all three of us then find myself driving in this
lovely little early seventies make-out muscle car
up some narrow gravel sort of winding suburban
coalmining upstate new york adirondack mountain
with ray manzereck from the doors to fool around
out of a sense of duty and obligation and purpose
and wanting to keep my word and promise but again
kind of conflicted cause knew deep down inside was
just not my true calling and sexual identity and guess
that's the thing about dreaming such a fine line between
the heart and the mind and when i woke up knew i was
really slightly in love with that bright-eyed girl in a sun
dress with the windy wild smile from one of those hope
ful pastel poloroid photos all the way back in childhood

American Hx: Act XXXXVII

One of those school crushes
like a sugar rush like a blood rush
was pure blissful empty vacant beauty
of love while your senses suddenly opened
and flooded and able to detect every little detailed
scent of nature from the ball field all the way down
to the river (that sensation of freedom) where you
might reveal feelings confessions and secrets

found out from her girlfriends
and the feeling was mutual
and returned the message

American Hx: Act XXXXVIII

After college i ran into my wet dream
while temporarily doing some door
manning in the upper east side.
she was living with some sort
of businessman schmuck
of a guy but as always was
real kind (if she only really
knew what went on behind
closed doors) this gorgeous
girl the daughter of a korean
diplomat while maybe it was
just in that collective unconscious
or in the air or some sort of spirit
but in one of those last classes
of high school in ap history while
for some reason standing i think
maybe strategically looking at
some map and taking notes
the whole time rubbing her
erogenous zones up against
me what else could i do but
to just stand there at attention
and feel titillated and honored
that she chose me to pleasantly
take full advantage (as if getting
closure and my wet dream cumming
to life) learning all about cold war russia

American Hx: Act XXXXIX

A couple *schwinn* bikes
              more than your
                            body weight
  than the density of man
            tossed in there
                    along with extra crates
                                of cel-ray soda & birch beer
     down in the bombshelter
               with enough downtime
                        to kill time
                              for a jewish boy
       as reformed as you can get
                  to dream about
                          theresa rodriguez
                                  the cuban bombshell

layup drills
laydown right
beside you with
no one to turn to
                pull-out beds
                    from the wall
                          to bawl
                              directions on how to do calesthetics
                         how to do cat's cradle how to do dance
                 steps how to duck under desks how to
         keep your wits about you how to howl

  put on those disguises
                for dose guys
                        who won't leave
                              you the hell alone
             come back home
                    when smell through
                            the floorboards
                                      supper
                of
      fish sticks
  & sloppy joe

American Hx: Act L

A moment in time when looking back at life
all that really mattered was a deep shag rug
a gigantic *crayola* leaned up in the corner of
the bedroom an old *zenith* tv with a sky-blue
screen a secret set of rear stairs in the back
of the kitchen heading to the upstairs hall
also a steep one leading to the attic dad's
stash of playboys fantasies of the daughter
next door the scent of suburban marigolds
and weeping willow which just kept on
growing and growing to the heavens
and saved our soul and in many
ways it did so perhaps that should
just be the thing we are shooting for

American Hx: Act LI

M. chagall just like che guevara
flies the friendly skies of florida
with his pawnshop harp and
hightop sneakers displaced
and damaged just looking
for a place to call his own
fluttering over all the synagogues
and stripmalls and dinner theaters
full of old timers and traveling actors
and right around the earlybird special
decides to descend and rest his bones
by one of those great big old banyan
trees only to discover they're swarming
with a whole flock of hobos and winos
and bums in a place they now refer to
as the 'stand your ground' state where
upstanding citizens wear their guns to
walmarts and nightclubs with a whole
new phenomenon and demarcation
called the hurricane season whole
cities on the gulf being eaten and
swallowed up by the rising sea
level but just like human nature
they all remain in denial with the
tide around their ankles and those
disney cruises taking off full of
spoiled brats who get half-off
with mickey and cinderella
waltzing around with their
chemical dependency problems
heading out to the higher-than-holy
all-inclusive horizon where during
happy hour get free drinks and wifi

American Hx: Act LII

Where are all those old friends you had
action-adventures with when you grew up
and always promised would get back to you?
did they get eaten up by the alligators in the swamp?
get into sword fights with borderline girlfriends claiming
their biting caustic rapier wit? or worst of all just become
something like actuaries accountants bankers used car
salesmen all pretty much in my opinion the exact same
people and conveniently at their own convenience never
getting back to you; something to say about all those
things that happened before that phase of puberty

American Hx: Act LIII

Back in the day when you were all by your lonesome
lost finally found in the madness & hustle & bustle
shuffle of it all somewhere in sweltering summer
of times square/hell's kitchen all you remember
were those lights and surreal signs that simply
read 'real butter' 'live women' as heaven was
just a room with air-conditioner in the village

American Hx: Act LIV

Sitting at that fold-out table
right by the window with
a simple transistor over
the alley just hearing
the wild wailing of
dominican boys
in the evening
as you and your
best friend roomy
from the bookstore
listened over the radio
to the election and another
corrupt decision down in
florida cause his brother
was the governor and
there was absolutely
nothing we could do
about it my roommate
getting his doctorate
in asian studies from
columbia university
and myself a masters
in social work at yeshiva
and guess all we could
really do was move on
surviving off fried plantain
and cerveza uptown
on 181st in washington
heights and falling in love
with that girl from the bronx
who still lived with her mom

American Hx: Act LV

I always like falling asleep to those ol' black & white
movie clips of mafia families; i don't know maybe
just sort of grounds me and helps me to remember
my days in brooklyn & queens & new york city
(they were sick but also something a bit sacred)
people forget all about dutch schultz, kid twist,
that dude who started vegas, while maybe in
a strange way, just made me feel a little less
lonesome, a certain type of poetic justice
somewhere between loving your mother
and misanthropic (a part of things with
a sense of belonging) sitting on your
midnight summer stoop in the fluttering
shadows; a thief eavesdropping on the wild
stirring shapes and forms which would suddenly
show up out of nowhere of a stillness and solitude
beyond compare having no place to go, but still
somehow perfectly content and keen and aware

falling fast asleep with a moon streaming through
window and a certain quietude that could not
be disturbed or observed in any one of those
cruel and cut-throat, dead end suburbs…

American Hx: Act LVI

What odd and strange obscure reasons
people put such credence into grandfather
clocks, wired, wound-up, trembling, tucked
into dusty, shadowy corners of their house
strategically, secretly stashed somewhere
in a side hall or silent stall in bleak seasonal
solitude of dysfunctional dens and living rooms
like forgotten museums no one ever really goes
to anymore, there till the tenuous, tragic end of
time, tongue-tied between reality and denial, like
some old-fashioned, wind-up timekeeper who like
clockwork very responsibly stands at his post just
'going through the motions' to try and wake us up
out of our soporific stupors whose monotonous tick-
tock routine and ritual ironically there to repair bleary-
eyed, beaten and battered, damaged souls, while one
wonders is it all just to subconsciously remind us of
our mortality and eavesdrop on time, and everything
that we might have traumatically lost somewhere down
the line punching the clock somewhere between heaven
and hell; those old gold tarnished pendulums pacing
themselves in it for the long haul; the fragile minutia
of minutes ticking meticulously till eternity; the gong
of brutal bells like the blast of bombs methodically going
off on the hour to suddenly shock and trigger us out of
our comas and sleepwalking realities to remind us of
what was and what will never be again; that convenient
creaking closet door with a key and keyhole and crawl
space for all long-lost phantoms and ghosts to reflect
and ruminate on what life and time has so callously
cruelly done to them but for whatever half-crazed holy
reason that beaming, brittle, antiquated grandfather
decides to hang around and make his rounds does
become something of a sound inanimate animated
member of the family whether you like him or not

..

American Hx: Act LVII

The old kind benign black dope addict
nodding-out over his buffer going round
and round and round in circles in the foyer

real nice guy and makes an honest living…

American Hx: Act LVIII

Did buddha go through as much bullshit as me? the infamous liberals who act so eloquent and softspoken but ironically pass instant judgment and totally unreliable, and more times than not flake-out on you the last second; think i'd rather have the crackhead thieves who steal the shovel from our barn; at least they'll get the job done…

American Hx: Act LIX

How about demographics for the bear population?
the infamous moose and deer? is there no one out
there trained to shoot the game warden (with an
attitude pretty much of i'll get to it when i get
to it) strap him on the rack on top of the car
and refer to him as straight-up road kill for
the basement storage freezer when your
acquaintances from the lake that being
the ice fisherman gym teacher selectman
dig into that warm winter stew and make
the astute comment–"tastes a little gamy"

American Hx: Act LX

Billy Corgan from "smashing pumpkins" pleaded
in that sweet softspoken song–"believe in me, believe…"
while i guess that's about the best we can hope for and dream

American Hx: Act LXI

One of the best things
i ever heard just coming
out of nowhere from
the head of the family
stabilization team
from cranston
rhode island
as one of our
best pals from
south boston
his dad
the dean
of discipline
was going out
with a dancer
in his thick
new england
accent–"you can't
marry a strip-pah"

it seemed so simple
but in fact much deeper

American Hx: Act LXII

Pornography & the secret art of advertising
chemical engineer who's a neat freak
climbs the rorshach tree with a set
of binoculars taking sneak peeks
at the daughter next door who
has a figure to die for and a
whole future ahead of her

he's well-respected in the association
and considered 'a good family man'

American Hx: Act LXIII

I don't know and please forgive me but always
seem to see these old timers in their convertibles
looking so miserable dead to the world lost and lonesome
without life or expression appearing drained from living
an empty ridiculous reality so driven and determined
while just not really having given a damn about their
fellow man or just that whole damn dysfunctional
family who eventually just got the better of them
or from like old money or inheriting it all from some
will and now absurdly overcompensating trying vainly
futilely to relive some childhood like ghosts who got
the better of them or some broken marriage or just
having given up on all that coping and surviving
from buddha madman suffering wondering
what batman & robin would have looked like
in their old age racing in their batmobile zooming
off to the promised land as in my opinion probably
so much more motivated and inspired as sincerely living
a life having contributed something productive and positive

American Hx: Act LXIV

White collar criminals and tycoons
(the philandering philanthropists)
used to waltz in ballrooms and
never was it questioned nor a
particular distinction made as
long it was all for the cause of
big business and progress (thee
amerikan way) oil and the railroad
for imperialism and exceptionalism
never get a second chance to make
a first impression even it means
subjugation of whole cultures up
on that great beacon on the hill…

American Hx: Act LXV

They said there was a time in amerika
where you could get so much more
for your dollar or if worked hard
enough could do better than your
mother and father; does this ancient
proverb also apply to that lazy cat who
just sits all day in the sunlit bay window keeping
an eye out on the dusty piano and knick-knacks?

Perhaps we shouldn't focus so much on this or that
and just let sleeping dogs lie and leave all those
fuzzy memories to their rightful owner…

American Hx: Act LXVI

My life is what has gradually
accumulated on my refrigerator
the alcoholic anti-semetic plumber
ari dorfman for creative carpentry
magnets for the green lantern
and wonder woman, jfk before
he was assassinated, nirvana
before suicidal tendencies;
the c.e.o.'s are taking over
on my television sounding
something like budhi co.
up 3.8% somewhere in
the faroff fictional land
of mad towering sky
scrapers in dubai

American Hx: Act LXVII

I still know husbands who roll blunts
taking secret tokes inside garages
to try and keep the mirage alive

American Hx: Act LXVIII

The demographic or percentage
or proportion of the population
found dead on memorial day
with a smile on their face
and hand still stuck
in guacamole dip

the neighbors from the homeowner's association
he has absolutely nothing in common with
completely unaware of it rivaling that old
expression–'if a tree falls in the forest'

American Hx: LXIX

They should make candles
with the scent of
mothballs
blintzes
dead flowers
kasha varnikas

American Hx: Act LXX

What i remember most of all in looking back
the best class i ever had was where you put
science experiments up on the sill of your
mother's kitchen peculiar prickly avocado
pits in little dixie cups of water sprouting
stalks rising to the heavens terrariums
whose anthropological scenarios in
converse sneaker boxes seemed like
brilliant keen reenactments of evolution
sometimes even different shaped
clattering colored glass with the sun
streaming through casting a whole cast
of colorful prisms whenever might be feeling
a bit down and out and situationally-depressed

American Hx: Act LXXI

Just say the names of
kids you grew up with
just picture their faces
sans memories
and moments
no criteria or criticism
or thought process
or judgment
(no rumors
or betrayal)
stay away from
such absurd obscure
statements like 'having
made it' or 'not made it'
while repeating this over
and over again in speech
pattern and cadence not
by coincidence ironically
has absolutely no meaning
or substance; the numbers
on the back of their jerseys
and phone numbers again
with no connection
this is our vision
our version
of paradise
and heaven

American Hx: Act LXXII

The good thing about death
is you're finally forgotten
like going into your
20th, 30th year of
marriage and know
deep down inside
under all the scar
tissue still loves
you still not getting
your sense of humor
and taking you
too seriously
and literally
your boy
hood baby
sitter the older
sister next door
the daughter of
an embezzler
taught you
to smoke
and you
choking
on a fresh
cup of milk
(funny i ran
into her several
years later and
asked me if i
wanted to do
bong hits
with her)
your parents
on a dinner
date your
dad the dentist
schmoozing
with the water
bed salesman

the wives
ole time
childhood
friends
from oceanside
long island
and *the gong
show* on television
convinced starsky
& hutch & charlie's
angels would some
how save your soul
a whole generation
run by *brille cream*
break-ins and how
many licks it would
take to get to the
center like a sun
going down dying
down over the slow
death dusk of suburbia
the purr of propellers
and muffled sound
of dogs disappearing
in the distance with
all that repetitive
excessive worrying
about a happily ever
after fictional future

American Hx: Act LXXIII

Out here they purchase pools
out of deals they made with
daughters and future divorcees—
i don't know for us in the summer
it was just listening to the dead's–
workingman's dead and neil young's
hypnotic, soothing, american indian
country-influenced "after the gold rush"
"down by the river" peddling bicycles
for miles in the baking sun along
the highway to hook up with pals
by the reservoir hoping you might
get some later on that night whether
dreaming or not not so much the point

American Hx: Act LXXIV

Spending that whole summer
dozing off in the sun in deep
plush grass of your backyard
brook babbling in background
nothing wrong with dreaming
about your future doing extra
reading— sherwood anderson's
"winesburg, ohio," irving stone's
"passions of the mind" and
doestoevsky's "crime and
punishment" spending days
caddying for rich obnoxious
wallstreeters and spending
your tips on bronx runs
to pick up dime bags
being something of
a romantic looking
bronzed & handsome
searching for first love
joe strummer of the clash
the smiths and the english beat

American Hx: Act LXXV

Ending up pool-hopping
wandering down deep
dark suburban streets
in our tighty-whities
and tennis sneakers
casually chatting
and bullshitting
with buddies
not caring
who the
hell saw us
(as if nothing
else mattered
and nothing
else did) after
hysterically
leaping off
other people's
diving boards
right before dawn

American Hx: Act LXXVI

Spending those long
sweltering summer
nights strewn out
on the floor of
the gymnasium
watching westerns
robert redford
& paul newman
being chased all
over the sierra-nevada's
("who are those guys!")
knowing they never had
a fighting chance but still
cracking jokes at their own expense

the pink panther
that clumsy casanova
secret agent creeping
out of the woodwork

American Hx: Act LXXVII

When is that stage of human growth and development
when you start smelling a little like your grandmother
from jamaica, queens with that brilliant, panoramic
view of the brokendown trainyard at sunset
who would still call your dad the dentist
when was taking his family on vacation
to the caribbean and have him paged
at *kennedy* (i guess being a bit lonely
or a control freak) cause didn't have
his exact itinerary, while as the story
apparently seems to go actually called
the president of the airlines; who had
all these connections with those toll
booth clerks and provided them fresh
free turkey breasts and home-baked
hamentashen and wave her on through
like some jewish mafia princess in her
long gold cadillac as she'd go barreling
down the bronx river parkway while
no one could keep up with her
heading to her grandson's play
about the revolutionary war singing
aloud–"who was the first to shed his
blood? crispus attucks! crispus attucks!"
and now find yourself just naturally sighing
aloud like gabe kaplan from *welcome back kotter*

American Hx: Act LXXVIII

How you used to dip your sister's tampons
in the toilet and watch them expand and toss
them out the window of *the jerusalem plaza*
watching them splatter all over the hoods
of tourist cars like a boy in the lower east
side dropping gi joe with his parachute
on a do or die mission into the alley
both hoping deep down inside might
save our souls or what would happen
or get some kind of reaction; your dad
still a rough and tough kid from brooklyn
threatening to jump over the counter and
kick the shit out of them claiming they
weren't giving us soap and towels

American Hx: Act LXXIX

[traveling.]

1,

99 after-dinner mints under an ivory-white pillow

2,

large salmon-color salmon on kitchenette counter

3,

a pink cruise ship enters the black sand shore

4,

milfs assuming different poses in the pool
to test if they still got the power to seduce

5,

you dream of those trained tigers mauling the tourists
and then gently letting them back out into the forest

6,

jumbo crosswords
bun-sized hotdogs

7,

doze off like a dope addict with heat stroke

8,

the discotheques measure the distance
between one's desperation and loneliness

9,

haunted pagodas in the aristocratic hills at sunset

10,

you fall in love with the girl with the deep
southern drawl kind and humble turning
down your covers and have son give
her all your extra change as 'a token
of your esteem' (symptoms of self-esteem)
and all other things in this life gone missing

11,

you see why men worship
them and willing to do battle

12,

all captured in the souvenir shop postcard carousel

13,

why they invented suburbia and a life of leisure

14,

piano lounges where sun-burned couples
can forget it all with convenient amnesia

15,

only when you fall asleep
to the flush of air-conditioning
do you know you're really in the holy land
of anonymity far away from all familiar forms of being

16,

looking out over whole historic cities and seas
always made you feel 'absolutely' nothing

American Hx: Act LXXX

Lunch will now be served
on the dream in the night
mare of the doll's eyes on
the veranda by that overflown
brook from childhood who could
talk circles around all the bullshit of idiots
& imbeciles— where are the masked cousins
& incestuous sisters whispering sweet-nothings
tongue-in-cheek as i find myself so fatigued
of the wicked whispering politicians & scholars
& king's men & queen's guards & got nothing
left to say to them (has anyone ever passed a
good rumor?) sometimes those dusty street
urchins playing soccer in the town square
the gypsies & gondoliers & tourists &
jesus christ not always in the right frame
of mind while i get all my news from
transistor radio of beautiful broke
down ancient cities teetering on white
washed precipices from the windchimes
from the whining seagulls & wild echo
of oceans & civilizations stirring in the
conch shell & the catcalls of a million
birds i know on a first name basis
the only ones trusted eavesdropping
outside my window who wake me up
& put me to sleep each & every night
to remind me to finally pick the
forgotten carrots & brussel sprouts
having survived november's garden

American Hx: Act LXXXI

When given the chance or opportunity
would always somehow find a way
to survive and thrive and get by
while totally overwhelmed by
living and this thing called life
(more specifically my internship
and the bullshit of social policy
and statistics) and when life was
just getting the better of me used
to get blowjobs from this borderline
divorcee in riverdale in the basement
of the yeshiva university library (like
some film noir where she seduced and
took advantage but kind of knew the
whole time what was going on cause
been around the block way too many
times and both in desperate need of a
good time or everything life had done
to us) listening to the female puerto rican
security guard who was always so tough
and hard, higher-than-holy, pissy, pissing
in her stall as i used to always get carded
and asked for my i.d. that much more cause
i was not orthodox and didn't wear the whole
get up and sort of funny and ironic when we
all graduated i turned out to be far more the
family man where they got caught (apparently
liking their new-found freedom) with their pants
down cheating and taking advantage after their
shifts at the mental health clinic with latino girls
over their personal computers and their wives
who thought they were committed, loyal and
loved them and menches asking them for divorces

American Hx: Act LXXXII

You can look back at some of the girls
you had and some of them sure as hell
had you and the things they did to you
but gotten to that point in my life where
i also like to look back at all those deli's
and those places that had the best pastrami
and chicken salad with curry and seafood salad
and calzones and eggplant parmesan while turns
out you're still just that kid on the back of that box
of *frosted flakes* licking his lips looking to be saved

old timers dragging *radioflyers* with
cases of beer through the blizzard…

American Hx: Act LXXXIII

All i need every day is that smooth-speaking dj
to comfort & cradle me to nurture & nature me
to soothe & whisper me sweet-nothings to bathe
& feed me chinese & whiskey & when we go
to sleep let me weep in her belly even laugh
a little shaking off all the bullshit of society
while things really haven't changed too much
for me since i was a teen wanting to fall asleep
to the static of the yankees on *wabc* radio; that
make me something of a lifetime dreamer getting
up in my sweat-stained underwear on the steaming
parquet floor of the 12th floor to the stray sounds
of sirens somewhere around midnight with insomnia
in *the john adams* on 12th st & 6th avenue full of
students & studs & divorcees & rich daughters
after smoking a j. midget wrestling muted on the
tv after spending a whole sweltering summer's day
reading *ullyses* on the rooftop now contemplating
the whole damn suffering universe in front of the
light of the refrigerator leftover tortellini & pesto

American Hx: Act LXXXIV

I swear to god to god i swear
it's never the crises that get to me
as that i can handle and get through
but just all the constant trivial bullshit
and cognitive disconnects and disrespect
complete lack of communication and follow
through from what we refer to as that species
of grownup and human (which to me sorry
to say the classic oxy/moron) that always
just makes you feel so damn alone while
ain't looking anymore for angels coming
down from the heavens but more so those
king's fools and buffoons with bells on…

American Hx: Act LXXXV

I'm sorry this is my apology letter not really
but why part of this plague and all of these
tv commercials are such bullshit to me how
domino's and *pizza hut* and *frito-lay* just
care so much about our health and welfare
and the new bumper sticker motto of–"we're
all in this together" (sort of like when neglectful
bp oil had their token oil spills and pretend like
a year or so later with their manipulation and
'secrets of advertising' convenient zombie
amnesia we would just forget it all and do
commercials pretending like they care so
much about the environment; *wells fargo*
warning us about scams and fraud) as when
it gets warm in america out come all the white
trash and white devils with their attention-seeking
motorcycles, taking off from runway 1, runway 2,
runway 3 while this loud bullying violating rumbling
noise pollution (america always with its compulsion
to control and take over and go marching off to war)
is supposed to represent something of individualism and
culture but could be nothing further from the truth, inaccurate
or opposite (with its pathetic plastic cookie-cutter conformist
mass-mentality fine line between prostitution and propaganda)
and couldn't think of anything more meant to drive you down
into the ground and steal your spirit and soul; all these crunchy
fake liberals and yuppies from hell with their fiberglass kayaks
and canoes (and *ski-doos* and 6 packs of beer) but what about
that whole forgotten culture of native-americans who you
annihilated and still keep hidden in the shadows out of sight
somewhere deep in no man's land on the great pains heartland

American Hx: Act LXXXVI

They always got these really weird fucked-up
fake proverbs to say like when those astronauts
blasted off to space during the late-sixties or even
right now on space x to meet their fellow colleagues
out in the space station as i find even more i cannot
relate, and when looking down at the planet earth
from space try to say all this real profound shit about
mankind and existence, while honestly if it was me
would not give a flying and just keep on going until
i didn't see planet earth at all anymore then really have
something deep to say about the whole truth of the matter

i can't explain why (well i can but i won't)
how i trust the child who constantly gets a bad rap
than that adult with the perfect impeccable reputation

American Hx: LXXXVII

A high school kid very focused and driven
goes to the mall to purchase more megabites
for his computer; i find myself lost as usual
searching for general tsau's chicken and
wonder if he had to fight similar battles

American Hx: LXXXVIII

Praise be to those ole time black & white
vaudevillian slapstick comedians who for
purposes of comedy & intimacy all slept
in the same big poverty-stricken great
depression bed laurel & hardy in their
sleep wear and the stooges all snoring
in unison while silly serious salesman
amerika busy building its great cities
& skyscrapers taking over the land

comedy teams where the sarcastic
salt-of-the-earth soul helped us
to get through it, worry just a
little less and lighten our load

American Hx: LXXXIX

I scene my hole life
pass in front of me
at the drive-in movie
found dead with a grin
during the change of
seasons finally resting
in peace (a cheeseburger
and onion rings; the only
time they want me is dead
or alive) like montgomery
cliff james dean in the weeds
with that large mean frauline
in the ticket booth still giving
me the evil eye don't know
why and take off with my
fiancée following the signs
with no sign of life back to
providence, rhode island…

American Hx: Act LXXXX

Letter To James Stewart & Katharine Hepburn
Humphrey Bogart & Edward G. Robinson:

When did our movie stars all become
action & adventure cartoon characters
with their perfect health club bodies
inherently knowing the ancient art
of karate & judo chops aerobically
running away the last second from
fireballs silhouetted by nightfall?

does anyone do film noir anymore?

in contemporary culture civilization
101 gotta be clark kent/man of steel
to not internalize (& become self-
destructive) the bullshit bureaucratic
soulless social system of stats & scams

by the time you 'get through'
already put a bullet in your head...

American Hx: Act LXXXXI

Can't seem to get out of my head
that childhood chant from summer
camp when back then played sports
like some sort of mythological hero
"six foot two, eyes are blue, richie
cohen is after you! six foot two,
eyes are blue, richie cohen
is after you! six foot two…"

American Hx: Act LXXXXII

You get to the moon and it's not blue but a
jigsaw puzzle just as i expected with pieces
missing here and there and being something
of a kid-thief-kleptomaniac always in crisis
showing great aptitude and potential for
acting-out and improvisation decide instead
to just head back to the planet earth for the hell
of it to a whole mess of aliens i could never ever
quite relate to, make much sense of, or any sort of
connection returning to a tiny absurd empty vacant
home just as i left it with the cheap floral furniture
all wrapped in plastic; that center piece of
wax fruit and my only companion the coo
coo coming out the wallpaper on the hour

fathers missing-in-action
swallowed in the hollow
mouth of the clown

brothers passed-out from
sniffing model glue
in the dryer

while myself sleeping
it all off in a room full of
wicked dolls from the old country

American Hx: Act LXXXXIII

Today in driving past the general store
over the gorge the church of the crucified one
to pick up perennials on the side of the mountain
i saw this small ranch perched up on top of a hill
with a little american flag whipping in the wind
an above ground pool and group of tombstones
and thought all we really need in this life is
a piece of land and piece of mind to get by

American Hx: Act LXXXXIV

It was the von trapps and there was this pretty
blonde-haired girl just sitting there in her cut-
off shorts with a mask on reading a book letting
the tourists in (the old men pathetically trying to
sweet talk her and her knowing exactly what she
was doing) while that image of just her sitting there
in her cut-off shorts and her long blonde hair simply
reading a book in more ways than nun meant the world

American Hx: Act LXXXXV

A thunderstorm falls on the theater
as all you hear is rumbling from
the thick verdant mountains, the
swollen rivers and red brick alley
of the village, while all that's left
is a simple soaked sundress dripping
on the line, which represents all of
tick-tock, lonely, seductive, solitary
time and existence with lazy languid
tugs drifting beneath distant bridges

American Hx: LXXXXVI

O to wake up to warm drizzle
in the misty mountains
and trees rising
to the clouds
of overcast
heavens

you can feel
your heart beating
and alive once again!

American Hx: Act LXXXXVII

a prayer for the mountains
a prayer for the sea
a prayer for the country
a prayer for the city
a prayer for you
a prayer for me
a prayer for the dusk
a prayer for the dawn
a prayer for the dew
a prayer for the lawn
a prayer for the stars
a prayer for the shore
a prayer for the runaway
a prayer for the rogue
a prayer for just somehow
finding your way back home

American Hx: Act LXXXXVIII

All that matters
is a true-blue girl
in her blue rodeo
peasant shirt who
believes in you in
the forget me not
blue evening of
upper west side
broadway and
a whole future
ahead of you

American Hx: Act LXXXXIX

To know the stars
are really just a drag
race through the flash
in neon after the movie
theater burns down and
rooster crows at dawn…

American Hx: Act C

A boxcar diner
which sits below
the silhouetted
mountain that
separates the
holy seasons
traintracks
& river
the tick-
tock village
yesterday
from to
morrow
truth
from
folk
lore
fear
& hope
romance
& love

American Hx: Act CI

Someday when this whole thing's over
we'll just eat fresh-baked crumbcake
straight out the oven with cups
of warm milk on the veranda
when the fishermen come
back from sea in the evening

only sound the buoys in the breeze...

#69

Before:

I remember back in the day sent away
for one of those kits from the back of a
comic 'cuz as a kid didn't want to be any
more a 79 lbs. weakling having sand kicked
in my face (guess that all-american advertising
touching on all the shame and insecurities and
collective unconscious of a boy in the throws
of puberty) and everyday with great heaps
of curiosity and gusto went back and forth
between my mailbox and home and it just
never showed up and somehow like every
thing else just learned to accept it and guess
should have realized this would end up being
the grand metaphor for all the bullshit (false
advertising) and emptiness of existence…

After:

Mad magazine won't stop writing and harassing me on my e-mail like once or twice a month telling me my son's subscription is up and without consent dipping into my account claiming they couldn't withdraw funds from my credit card because it is void as ironically this is the shit and fucked-up things that satire is made of (usually some form of abuse of power from up above or violation or invasion of privacy from the lovely adult world) mad magazine who won't stop writing me nonstop with those pre-manufactured computerized e-mails which say "no reply" (when these are the swine writing me and i sure as hell never gave them the ok to just randomly charge my card whenever they wanted! is this what the better business bureau is for? why all those ancient ancestors started yiddish to get all that shit off their chest using such secretive cryptic dialect like "scheister" and "shylock" and "schmendrick") all those things you find so offensive and ironically completely maddening and pure madness while just wanted to supply my kid some good satire and wonder what the fuck happened to the good ole times thinking of writing a letter to sir al fred j neuman…

#70

Woke up this morning to the light of the cooking channel
and it was patti labelle and curtis "50 cent" jackson
the queen's rapper who took like 7 to the chest and
survived it and was wearing a nice holiday sweater
and when went to commercial affectionately put
his hand on patti's shoulder and it's just things
like this (50 cent hanging out in patti labelle's
kitchen) not necessarily julia child or all the
phony hoity-toities out in the hamptons that
inspires me to get up and into the shower

#71

Your wife writes you during the day
simply asking if you're taking care of yourself
pathetically i see this as something of a love letter

#72

if p:

Later on during the weekend, fooling around a little
when driving with her and the kid find myself singing
"your love is like oxygen, you get too much, you get
too high, not enough and you're gonna die." i tell her
that's by *air supply* and she rolls her eyes then happen
to mention she's got cute toes (years ago she would
have felt flattered and glowed) now she gives me a
look like i'm trying to take advantage of her, my kid
takes my side as knows i'm really a romantic at heart

god bless him for that…

then q:

Whenever marriage is driving me up the wall
when they make absolutely no sense at all
i find myself just naturally singing the song
"and i don't need some pretty face to tell
me pretty lies, all i need is someone to believe"
as if some spiritual trigger to the damaged psyche
feeling practically the same thing at the age of 53
as i did at the age of 13; billie joel's masterpiece
"the stranger" coming out some time around the
late 70's i picked up at *the white plains mall* and
when i got it home played it over and over again
until it became part of my soul and no one could
do me wrong, while that's the thing about great
music about great songs and all the things it can
do for you and how it can even actually heal you
all those maddening things and girls in between

#73

proposition 1:

With war you name them— revolutionary, the civil war korea, vietnam, iraq, afghanistan, it was always about coming back to the wife, to the girl you loved (those starlets who got pinned-up in the bunker claiming this is who you were fighting for) even when they didn't make that space mission by absolutely no fault of their own as in apollo 13 all the courageous things they had to do to stay alive and get by and get home to the wife when those 3 real smart and humble and self-effacing astronauts back in the day when they were still real 'down to earth' and modest in buzzed haircuts answered all those *nasa s*pace questions they ended the conference with the one in the middle having to respond to how he's now the most eligible bachelor in america and everyone cracked-up and said let's end it on that; end it always with such facts like when chris rock did his brilliant world tour comedy act he spoke about the fact about how after nelson mandela got locked up for decades on end, even tortured by his captors only after a couple months of being home had to get a divorce cause just couldn't take it anymore so i suppose the real profound operational question should more so be about all those necessary strategies and coping and survival mechanisms and skills of kill or be killed in the holy bond of matrimony ritual and ceremony we so casually refer to as marriage proposition 2:

It's kind of funny but when guys grow up and get married that girl they fell madly in love with becomes a nudge (ironically ends up driving them crazy) constantly kvetching and complaining they need to clean up after themselves ending up resembling a little bit their mothers, and might see why some guys turn to drinking and cheating as some desperate form of acting-out and rebelling, subconsciously or even consciously (as sure as heck don't need this type of guidance, couldn't stand it in the first place…) futilely trying to assert their independence and become more complete

proposition 3:

He who survives marriage or for that matter blindly abides by
it is a slave in some form or another; to the theater of the absurd
and often the biggest punk of perverse proportions; the dummy
and ventriloquist swapping disguises, going back and forth in
a ruthless, futile power-struggle which has no light at the end
of the tunnel (after you have a child seems like you're always
put on trial) not sure whether to hand her a bouquet of burning
flowers or just blow your brains out (a victim of the predictable
and obvious) both seem just as accurate and viable alternatives
and the grand punchline to this all too ridiculous tragedy of petty
bickering, rules and regulations, routines and rituals in a reality
bent to steal all passion and spontaneity, and forget the original
romantic reason to why you even decided to walk down the aisle
in the first place, as all those so-called pals and acquaintances
and resentful relatives with their crooked smiles looked on
sardonically, like getting advice from a two-faced thief

the origins of slapstick and drinking
will this day, will this life ever end?

proof:

Falling in love is like some dress rehearsal
for not knowing what's to come in the future

proof:

The snow slashes so filthy in the suburbs
when you are a kid and feel like you got
no one to turn to (where is everyone?)
and friends worse than any grownup
you ever knew i mean not like anything
you pictured in being a kid while looking
back like some sort of surreal existential
nightmare or some surprise party where
they stay hidden behind the furniture...

proof:

It's weird i know i've saved so many peers and acquaintances—
a matter of fact they'll even mention it just a bit later, then ironically
never ever hear from them again (or at times even the first ones to try
and do you in) that feeling of what it feels to be absolutely anonymous

proof:

The angry drunk
takes lunch with
the happy monk
only to find out
how much they
actually have
in common
and very
much
cut from
the same cloth
and how easily
could just swap
roles and emotions
and how that bullshit
expression–"i'm sure
we know a lot of
the same people"
feels so apropos

proof:

"Dylan bring your buddhist bible"
"Mom wants me to study
 my driver's manual…"
 buddhist bible, driver's manual
 and with episodes of insomnia
 you fall asleep to old reruns
 of *the fugitive*, incredible
 52 weeks a year and
 had like a 4 year run
 pretty much about this
 doctor on-the-run accused
 of a crime he was not guilty of
 and almost every one ends like
 showing him ducking behind some
 superman phone booth sparking
 a cigarette under some fedora
 and find really able to connect
 and content seeming something
 between a dream and nightmare

proof:

The workaholics all have perfect yards
but you never see anyone on them
except for the gardeners like adding
fertilizer to some absurd bizarre illusion

beware and be careful in taking a stroll
as may very well be viewed as suspicious
alarms go off in the mansions and
they bring you in for questioning

proof:

Where's my getaway car? seems like still
in garage trying to pay off on layaway plan

#74

You can talk about guys (i'd rather not…)
but women's emotions appear so much more
primitive & raw & only begin to really understand
them until about a day & a half later when all that
guilt starts to kick in. i guess there was a reason
with the hx of civilization why they invented
the roman coliseum; those game shows asking
some poor soul what's behind curtain #1 curtain
#2 curtain #3 which know in the long-run none of
it really matters or means a thing, while all some
pretty placating shit to hope to provide an instant
panacea or cure the emptiness of the studio audience
& all those lost lonesome viewers out there in tv land
for one reason or another made the wrong choice in men

#75

The weather woman i really like is out again on maternity leave
think that makes like the 47,632 time in the last couple of weeks
and think something fishy may be going on as all they show now
is one of those great big nondescript condos along the gulf coast
and say we're expected to get pounded by heavy wind and rain

tell me something i don't know
and think might be suffering from
one of those situational depressions…

#76

I'm a sicko and imagine her giving birth to me
then cuddling and spooning in her vaginal
discharge bathed by the light of television

the ultimate room service pillow talk
do not disturb the end happily ever after…

#77

Whose idea was it to name those tropical storms?
think it would have been so much more descriptive and
apropos if they did yiddish like poop schmeer & oy gevalt

Guest Notes:

guest requests a pina-colada be brought to room every night
at the bewitching hour some time between 4:30 and 5:00

guest requests lounge act drops by asking for advice and might
actually take it like the wife once did during honeymoon period

guest requests unconditional kindness and compassion
as claims down here everyone wants a piece of him

not sure who to turn to
god or jesus?

guest requests two bagels with cream cheese and lox, a red onion
and capers, bag of sour cream & onion potato chips and dill pickle

guest requests it's brought by a nice and kind, thoughtful
puerto rican who will turn down his bed with him still in it

guest requests like a pretty stewardess who does whole shtick
with inflatable vest and oxygen mask may religiously ask

about the status of do not disturb sign and repeatedly
point to the outside to keep out all of evil mankind

guest requests she softly unwraps the wrapper of after-dinner mint
and place it gently in his mouth like a preacher during confession

guest requests no small talk of any sorts and will put
tip in envelope and place respectfully in her uniform

guest requests if seems to be feening or fixating
don't pay him any mind and leave him be

that's what the pina-colada
and self-medicating are for

guest requests she asks if anything
else need be done in native tongue...

A Sonnet Called Do Not Disturb

Shakespeare— all that bullshit & betrayal
you must have gone through and had to
endure? heard where you were from
were not just assassins of character
but real-life executioners to back it up
as life must have just seemed like one big
con constantly on-the-run having to watch
your back (tragedy & satire & such a fine line
between passion & paranoia, promises & poison,
fate & coincidence, politics & survival of the fittest)
moon still hangs like a delicate pin cushion in the early
morning sky over bleary-eyed motel in the berkshires
next to a revolutionary war graveyard and the piping
smokestacks of factories on the river, and even
though you're just barely hanging on in constant
crisis nothing makes you feel more alive, grasping
onto the wisps of lingering spirits, as it is clear
everything just lasts in the moment, and the past
and the future just a brilliant fleeting grand illusion
while will love & hate you for the exact same reasons

#78

After the torrents of rain
used to fall down outside
our house and fill in the gaps
of that dried-up empty brook
it felt like a true-blue river whose
currents brought life and character
to our monotonous melancholic
brooding being getting things
going again breaking through
all those broke down ruins
that for no particular reason
stagnate and slow us down
all those worries and concerns
at last leaping in a linear manner
to some long-lost final destiny
not caring or giving a damn
where it ended and for this
exact reason feeling the instant
sensation of freedom and sense
of redemption hurtling in leaps
and bounds with a wild uncontrollable
insane rage through patches of ancient
pachysandra escaping towards the eternal
folklore of the blissful roar of the unknown

#79

Getting ready for the apocalypse
i suppose is very much like getting
ready for a hurricane for the insane
rains for getting out your change of
season clothing for a reunion with
a real old pal acquaintance for a past
mad girlfriend of passion of betrayal
and broken promises for a surprise
party at your funeral for going back
on vacation to paris, israel, antigua,
andalucia for this time crossing the
strait of gibralter maybe making it
up to madrid or basque country…

#80

How to make
monkey bread
polenta, and a
name for yourself

#81

You imagine yourself just sitting back
on some splendid makeshift raft with
an eternal never ending wraparound
porch reading proust till your heart's
content, stepping inside when you get
sick of it all, crestfallen, down on your
luck resembling one of those conch shells
empty and hollow; the out-of-work actors
(the real saints & studs) going at the surf
& turf platter. you feel most comfortable
around them 'cause know they're just as
deserted and abandoned lacking in direction
and just like you, don't really have a home...

#82

Those ole time home movies told all…
like some classic brilliant buster keaton
silent film playing it modest & humble
docile, deadpan, and down in the dumps

slapstick, self-destructive (life imitating art)
and couldn't help but be sympathetic
to this self-fulfilling prophet…

#83

I think we lived in a far better world
when the gigolos said such stuff like
wanted to leave a good looking corpse
as opposed to that whole breed of yuppie
schmuck, snapping papers maliciously on
the train, hostile, higher-than-holy, pretending
like the whole world revolves around them
mean-spirited and indifferent, like the
opposite of–'i think therefore i am'

proof:

You remember back in the eighties when they
had those things called power lunches (oy vey
ya gotta be kidding! and what exactly do you
do and what are you supposed to say, i mean
when you meet for one of these infamous power
lunches? do you take power leaks and power
shits as well? do you hook up with the perfect
power female to make the perfect power team
like something out of *d.c. comics*?) and you
wonder why we've always kind of not been
respected or resented, and even culturally
hated around the world (although our self-
absorbed egos would like to have you think
differently and that we are so loved) there's
this obscure tradition and phenomenon how
americans hate the french (well right back
at you!) i'll take any day petite-dejeuner
(power not necessary) meeting lover with a
bottle of rose for an hour and a half on le seine

#84

You imagine past girlfriends coming back to life
like one of those psychotic dolls but when they
see me feel so bad actually don't follow through
to cause me harm but just start to vacuum
and go back to their old ways of nagging

you wish they'd go with their original instincts…

#85

You used to love to take showers with them (maybe due to being alone for so long and appreciating them that much more) while simply going through their innocent girl grooming rituals shampooing conditioner over and over again like you weren't even there just standing there like some turned-on innocent bystander voyeur…

#86

Those days where we'd just listen to meatloaf's "bat out of hell"
porno for pyros, gustave mahler, ella fitzgerald & ole satchmo

foghorns right outside our window
leftover fried calamari in refrigerator

#87

A whole clothesline full of sagging soaking bras
outside my window of the ballerina in brooklyn

dripping hypnotic like some real-life she loves
me she loves me not ultimatum psychodrama

you had this great natural conversation running
into her coming out the subway from manhattan

and only upon reflection, looking back, were
you able to capture this offering and seduction

#88

To know everything starts from the middle
and the beginning has no end like a tug gliding
through foghorns appearing to have no destination

#89

Rimbaud #1 on the billboard charts
after he went solo sick of playing
second fiddle & role-reversal
& broke up with verlaines &
moved to far rockaway queens
right next to that brick church
growing out of the weeds
& all-night diner full of
drag queens & feening
dope addicts strolling
home with brown paper
bag full of pastrami
& stuffed derma
beneath the budding
cleveland pear blossom
to his beautiful burntdown
porthole pothole penthouse
under the stars with a view
of all those yentas in mock
fur gossiping to keep warm
& black boys doing back
flips off the boardwalk
& leftover porn stars
& vaudeville rappers
beneath the misty lamp
light on the corner of
the boulevard & ocean
where columbus in drag
drifts in with his bastard
brothers from barcelona

#90

All of culture and civilization began
from oliver twist's simple question
"please sir, may i have some mo?"
to the basic offer and support of–
"when you're a jet, you're a jet all
the way, from your first cigarette
to your last dying day" to jimi
after his mesmerizing guitar
solo of 'there's a red house
over yonder' who just
happens to mention
"awe shucks"

#91

When all you ever really needed was just
some small slapstick screwball scene some
thing straight out of *the stooges* not too
screwed up in the head due to what booze
and life does to them and your fine kind ole
timer alchie paratrooper boss one of the few
people you could actually rely on and trust
and if you yourself could prove to be reliable
and trustworthy and show up on a daily basis
and not make bullshit excuses at the end of
the day polish off a couple cases in basements
breaking down the day and existence cracking
up with a couple crazy one-liners and slowly
swerve home feeling a sense of belonging
and accomplishment while at week's end
a wad of straight-up cash under the table

#92

I.

I remember when i used to live
at *the jack london* in the dregs
of portland, oregon but still
tried to manage to find ways
of getting cultured and would
take buses on miserable blue
sunday afternoons over industrial
bridges out of town down bleak
suburban avenues which felt
like the end of the world
a nomad in no man's land
to catch matinees like "dances
with wolves" and when i got
out of the theater felt some
thing like a revelation like
i had been transformed
to a whole other era
and the rain would always
come down and tried to
make that feeling and
spirit last as long as i
could and then always
have to return to my
hole in the wall with
all those tribal dances
pounding howling
echoing running
through my blood
through my brain
my heart & soul

II.

I remember those days
summers in the big city
10th, 11th avenue hell's
kitchen, the $2 theater
where you'd sneak in
and watch movies all
day in the air-condition
hudson st. in the village
dazed, disoriented from
the heat, wandering all
alone through the sweltering
cobblestone literally could
feel and smell the melting
tar smoking below the holes
in the soles of my sneakers
bad boys with hearts of gold
playing ball in the asphalt park
suddenly sliding into second
and like some mock brawl
the whole team piling on
top of him wild and hysterical
some half-crazed kid scaling
the center field fence howling
and just that simple billboard
towering up above on the ave
which at the time seemed to
mean so much and say it all–
"don't forget the zip code"

III.

Taking a whore bath
with the prostitutes
wild hysterical then
(a bar of *lava s*oap
& shampoo included)
at the moment felt like
a revelation now seems
something of a dream
93 degrees, new york city
wandering down jane street
to the hudson having dropped
out of college but self-educating
myself and reading so much more
poetry & philosophy to me's what
was making a name for myself…

the drag queens coming out at dusk

IV.

They say what doesn't kill you makes you stronger
(yeah— maybe that be the case) but what if so much
goddamn trauma ain't even aware you're living no mo

i swear i've seen lumberjacks those just out of jail
the toughest and hardest working on the crew and that exact
evening literally strewn out on the curb disoriented and drunk

brothers from another mother
while we're all just a bunch of
punks trying to get by and make it

V.

Life & times
of a starfish
who can lose
an appendage
and it just naturally
grows back perfect
(gossip & rumors
what distinguishes
man from the wild
animal what makes
him subhuman)
regeneration
the only thing
i've ever wished

VI.

Man i wonder what it would be like to become famous
after you kick the bucket some pretty fucked-up shit
to suffer and struggle your whole existence and
then right when you bite the dust all the intellects
decide to come out of the woodwork and discover
all your brilliant work (like the dreams of a taxi-
dermist who prefers you pleasantly posthumous)
like what horrifically happened to van gogh and
kafka and think maybe even fyodor dostoevsky.
there's this psychological theory which i forgot
exactly what it means but believe even named
after one of the characters out of a mark twain
story when tom and huck come back from missing
after days of being out on the mississippi and think
they may have even dredged the river for them and
all their friends and family and acquaintances convinced
they are dead start expressing their deepest sense of remorse
and regret mourning hysterically at the ceremony as they
all of sudden show up like ghosts out of nowhere and ex-
perience their own funeral (like some form of disassociative
fugue which clinically implies how you get to your destination
but have absolutely no idea how you got there or possibly even
disassociating while somehow simultaneously being spiritually
connected) forgot exact psychological principle this applies to

The first thing they show on the morning news
is how two cruise ships collided into each other
(seems to have become something of a tradition)
leaving them twisted, smashed-up, then the ditsy
broadcaster with an ear to ear *dentyne* smile and
a caption which reads "things to do this weekend"

VII.

With mankind there is this ridiculous paradox and irony
of 'the tourist' when they try so desperately to be more
cultured, yet because of their aggressive, 'vulture-like'
ways (unable to avoid the herd mentality) end up
appearing and giving off the resemblance in being
so much less independent and individualistic, as
absurdly actually alienating and engulfing 'the native'
of that environment (treating them like slaves and sub-
servient, and will even act offended if don't adopt and
take on that expected role of acclimating and acculturating
to their own dreams and desires) in their desperate wish
to be eternally included and wanted and establish a sense
of belonging (all at the 'expense' and sacrifice and spirit
of others) seen as 'cultured' (but doing nothing to earn
it accruing materialistic items) while ironically only
end up so much more conformist due to the rude
(self-absorbed, exclusive, aloof and arrogant)
vulgar traits and characteristics and erratic
moods and behavior of human nature

VIII.

If they are not there for you spiritually
or at least mind, body, spirit and soul
(you choose one or all of the above)
almost prefer they're not there at all

fell in love with her at yeshiva
with an elevator full of rebbes
all joking-like, exclaiming–

"i'm gonna get you back for
fooling around with my sister!"

IX.

Even those weddings and
funerals do become political
that's the good thing about birth
purely spontaneous and spiritual
having absolutely nothing to do
with such petty hypocrisies and
contradictions that rule and regulate
(the self-interest of) human nature

how often the term 'rebirth'
is taken out of context...

X.

Father kept wept
content in broom closet
with kabbalah buddhist bible
black bread butter bottles
of wine celery soda seltzer
his weather radio which
will tell the time of tides
ice storms right around
erie duluth grand rapids

XI.

Jesus burned at the stake
staked to the wheel
in front of the hole
live studio audience
spun round and round
on the spinning wheel
where it stops nobody
knows on the everything
must go game show might
land on a vacation to hawaii
a cruise to the bahamas
a brand new set of furniture
set of luggage and if lands
in the wrong area in no
man's land just walk
out on him as they
cancel the show
going into instant
denial forgetting
pretending like nothing
ever happened the spring
board solstice for all of
culture & civilization

XII.

One wonders why *jeopardy*
always asks such random
questions like who
was rudyard kipling
and after you find
out who was rudyard
kipling still don't really
know a thing about him
(like i don't know
stephen daedalus
or even myself)
followed by
all these political
correct bullshit
commercials
about buzzed
drinking that
somehow buzzed
drinking is still
drinking but wasn't
that the whole point
to get buzzed while
drinking as for me
always drove so
much better and
more slow and
focused and keen
while drifting past
suburban seas
contemplating
reality where
when i got home
trying to keep
that buzz going
from my mom's
leftover wine in
the refrigerator
lounging back
in the den by
the big window

over the peaceful
river reading kerouac not
necessarily rudyard kipling

XIII.

As if getting reincarnated
from the ashes of a burnt
down bed & breakfast
witch once housed
george washington
a slice of warm
pecan pie after
dinner brandy
candle and
scriptures

XIV.

The rumble of thunder rolling in over the lake
just after we finished up our surprise feast of
hamburgers & fries & perfectly square slices
of vanilla cake all made by the winos brought
in from the bowery over the summer lying our
skinny bones down in the bunk waiting to whip
out our flashlights & archie & veronica comics
the sporting news to keep up with every statistic
of every player wearing mets & yankees uniforms

XV.

That series joe morgan
who played second base
for the big red machine had
johnny bench cesar geronimo

don't forget of course cat
fish hunter thurman munson
and mick "the quick" rivers
for the infamous bronx bombers

the path to the kingdom
seemed to lie somewhere
between nyc and cincinatti

XVI.

*

we start thinking most about our mortality
when things start repeating them
selves for all the wrong reasons

*

(all the things
that people *don't*
do that tests our faith)

*

let no man decide your fate as assure you
the laziest and biggest mistake you'll ever make

*

doesn't life just sometimes seem
like some self-fulfilling prophecy
from a whole other reality?

*

'the will of the people' is something
of an oxymoron when we got our backs up
against the wall forced to face our mortality

*

i can't roam down
any of these lone
some roads no mo'

#93

The real world the real world the real world the real world
there's a reason why the philosophers over time devoted
their lives in trying to find and discover (the meaning
behind) that quintessential or unadulterated pure and
'real world' (coming up with such mythological fables
of atlantis, or contemplating the rise and fall of the greek
and roman empires; the influence of the ancient egyptians)
but ironically, due to all the see-through hypocrisies and
contradictions of human nature, constantly, intensely,
obsessively had the need to keep on going back to it
(like the psychological nature and dynamic of the cycle
of abuse) finding it's all just an illusion, a state of mind
mood you're in (and that thing or definition does not exist)
and probably best to just remain slightly on the periphery
(on the outside looking in) with those few you believe
you think you might be able to trust respect and love

#94

That expression when you offer to make a cup of joe–
"how do you like it?" wouldn't it be great if could
simply apply this to existence and maybe all that
it is is just hugs and kisses, or one mad rapturous
one in the chaos of it all which instantly cures all
and separates all the bullshit from the folklore
with the sensation of finally heading home
whatever or wherever that happens to be?

#95

They say during that period of the arab spring
many of the young people didn't know where
to meet for the revolution and rallies 'cause
the government turned off their wifi service
oy vey! did they forget the fight for algiers?

#96

The pretty, pale, red-haired broadcaster
from *bbc* news daintily points to the big
screen which reads–"venice flooding"
while flocks of idiot smiling tourist
families take selfies of themselves
knee-deep in front of ancient cathedrals
completely oblivious to global warming.
i guess this is the best that can be expected
for civilization 101, while you sip from your
cumberland farm coffee brooding about the
upcoming holiday season of consumerism

#97

You see why old timers spend the rest of their days
in dim basements contented like mad scientists
hunched over their stamp and coin collections

#98

The birdman of alcatraz seemed
to have the right idea turning over
a new leaf and sending his pigeons out
on secret missions all for the sake of man

proof:

I am an owl
who has lost
its howl
so have be
come some
thing of
a wise
ass
hoping
some
one
will
listen

#99

How the call of a crow
just as placating and soulful
as the tick-tock of a clock
as the windy wild apples
dropping to the sidewalk

as the train drifting
into delicate mist
of the wisps
of fall foliage
factory mountains

#100

Chugging away past the hitch hikers of the villages and rivers… past that sadistic state cop who got taken off his beat for roughing up the innocent bystanders of the community and now sits secretly on his bike in the alley seething, stoic, trying to look all tough in bike helmet, a whistle in his smug mug and very sexy short shorts. past the short-order cook roaming home exhausted and pretty girls from the hardware store having put old timers under their spell. past those angels in sundresses who just can't seem to find the right man to take care of them and now spend their days and dusks wandering on library lawns very studiously, meticulously picking up scattered acorns. past bad boy studs getting their werewolf beards buzzed by old man barbers who seem like the only ones who can understand and relate to them and been through the exact same thing as them

#101

A bleak sun peeking through pekid clouds
provides some sort of trigger to one of those
split-rail fences in childhood suburbs; that neighbor
who once exposed herself to me i ran into several years
later who i already spoke about and knew had seen her
fair share of living i guess with a similar arrested stage
of development asking me if i wanted to do some bong
hits up in her parent's condo in the upper east side

i just casually said no that will be alright
as just knew would lead to way too serious
things while satisfied with the long eternal sigh

like milk bottles left outside
getting filled with downpour
from a whole other time...

Denouement:

*

Where is that mythological god of the fog
                                        horns?
imagine he'd look a lot like miles
with his back turned from the crowd
blowing some long slow psalm
getting them through the storm
fishermen return from tour
for their bundle of heroin

*

How about some sort of mythological god
who balances the burden of the great
glowing sun up on his shoulders
climbing up that long steep
suburban hill to work for
some old ungrateful
obnoxious widow
or customers who
treat him and make
him feel like a 'complete
stranger' and day in and day
out just finds gratitude in his
chinese take-out appreciating
every last single bite in his long
lost lonesome welfare hotel room
repeating this routine and ritual
showing up making no excuses
day in day out on a daily basis?

*

The log trucks keep on rolling
back & forth from the mountain
which ironically somehow seems

to ground you; this life gets so damn
draining and the snow keeps on falling

When do you start turning
to whiskey, jugs of sangria
writing letters to tell her you
still love her and sorry how it
ended, ending up lonelier than
the original reason you got together

*

You think maybe eventually it really just is all that loneliness
that gets you in the end, like the crooked pictures on the wall
of some widow's inn curator of a wax museum just going through
the motions mona lisa's jigsaw puzzle tooth falling out of her grin

*

Who is gonna read me my stanzas on my deathbed
having no idea who i am but still wanting to make
edits as if this would make some sort of difference
leaving the blinds open just a slight bit to catch
the image of that skywriter leaving its chalk-white
trail of fairy dust against the bright blue sky turning
to a squiggly line when it heads right down straight
into the center of the sun while in my backyard hear
the chattering of birds and the distant childhood familiar
hum of lawnmowers fading into the dying day those half
crazed angels blindfolded being spun round and round
dizzy disoriented staggering over to the pinata feening
futilely taking swings at its internal organs hoping for all
candied insides to just spill out onto the plush lawn their
own version of the pot of gold at the end of the rainbow

*

And like buddha devoid of all fear and
hope everything fading into the dusk...

Joseph Reich is a social worker who lives with his wife and fourteen-year old son in the high-up mountains of Vermont.

He has been published in a wide variety of eclectic literary journals both here and abroad, been nominated seven times for The Pushcart Prize, and has written over twenty books of poetry and cultural studies.

He wholeheartedly agrees with Voltaire and Neil Young that man needs a maid, and still trying to make his way through *Finnegan's Wake*.

www.ingramcontent.com/pod-product-compliance
Lightning Source LLC
Chambersburg PA
CBHW030850170426
43193CB00009BA/556